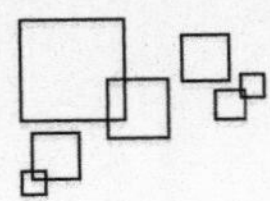

Bible Brain Builders, Volume 3

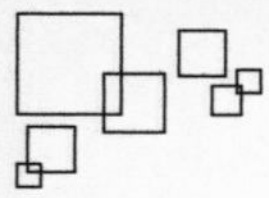

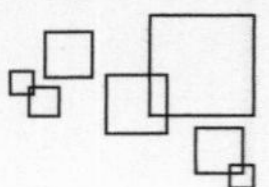

Other Bible Brain Builders

Bible Brain Builders, Volume 1

Bible Brain Builders, Volume 2

Bible Brain Builders, Volume 4

Bible Brain Builders, Volume 5

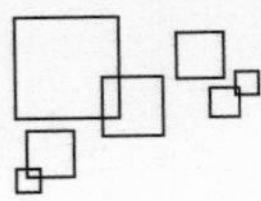

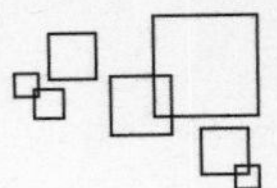

Bible Brain Builders

Volume 3

THOMAS NELSON
Since 1798

NASHVILLE DALLAS MEXICO CITY RIO DE JANEIRO

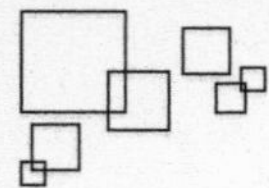

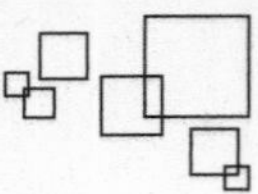

Published in Nashville, Tennessee, by Thomas Nelson. Thomas Nelson is a registered trademark of Thomas Nelson, Inc.

Book design and composition by Graphic World, Inc.

Original puzzles and mazes created by W. B. Freeman.

Thomas Nelson, Inc., titles may be purchased in bulk for educational, business, fund-raising, or sales promotional use. For information, please e-mail SpecialMarkets@ThomasNelson.com.

ISBN: 978-1-4185-4914-5

Printed in Mexico

14 13 12 11 QG 1 2 3 4 5 6

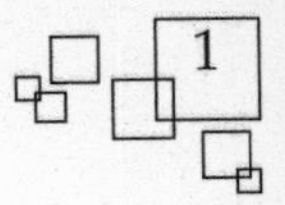

Eyewitnesses

On their way to the tomb that Easter morning, the women wondered how they would roll away the stone so they could anoint the body of Jesus with spices and oil. Little did they realize they were soon to be eyewitnesses to the greatest event in history. The Gospel accounts differ as to who was in that early-morning group, but there is no dispute as to the significance of the event—Jesus, Son of God, was dead and is alive again! Death has been overcome!

Start

End

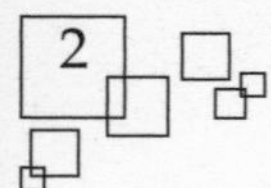

*T*he people of the Bible appreciated oil because of its many practical and spiritual uses, but they had a love-hate relationship with vinegar. This puzzle illuminates some of the uses and abuses of these precious liquids.

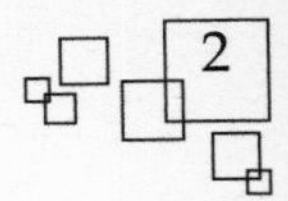

Across

5 Job's steps were once bathed with this milky liquid, while the rock poured out rivers of oil (Job 29:6)

6 Taking away this piece of apparel is like vinegar on soda, says Proverbs (Proverbs 25:20)

10 The psalmist was anointed with "new" oil (Psalm 92:10)

11 Taking the vow of one of these meant drinking no vinegar made from wine (Numbers 6:2–3)

15 In Exodus, the lamp burned with oil made from pressed ____ (Exodus 27:20)

16 They put sour wine on one of these and gave it to Jesus to drink (Matthew 27:48)

20 Luke says they mocked Jesus when they offered Him sour wine (Luke 23:36)

21 The woman poured costly oil on this part of Jesus' body (Mark 14:3)

23 These unleavened items (sing.) made of wheat flour were anointed with oil (Exodus 29:2)

24 He anointed the original tabernacle with oil (Leviticus 8:10)

25 These are with us always; His anointing was therefore proper (Mark 14:7)

Down

1 His servant lowered a debtor's bill to 50 measures of oil (2 words) (Luke 16:1–6)

2 #11 Across couldn't drink this fruit juice (Numbers 6:3)

3 Smoke to the eyes is like vinegar to these (Proverbs 10:26)

4 These altar "implements" were also anointed with oil (Leviticus 8:11)

7 She dipped her bread in vinegar at Boaz's table (Ruth 2:8, 14)

8 In John, Mary anointed Jesus' feet with this costly oil (John 12:3)

9 The "ill" should be anointed with oil (James 5:14)

10 The oil used in #21 Across was "pleasantly scented" (Mark 14:4)

12 David's "enemies" gave him vinegar to drink (Psalm 69:19, 21)

13 Two hundred and fifty shekels of this (sugar's "source") were used in the holy anointing oil (Exodus 30:23)

14 Timely rain meant the people could gather oil and "cereal" (Deuteronomy 11:14)

17 Some were foolish and some were wise as they took their lamps to meet the bridegroom (Matthew 25:1–4)

18 Jesus was anointed with this oil of "happiness" more than His companions (Hebrews 1:9)

19 The third item that could be gathered, from #14 Down (2 words) (Deuteronomy 11:14)

21 The type of plant used to convey sour wine to Jesus on the cross (John 19:29)

22 Moses sprinkled oil on this seven times to sanctify it (Leviticus 8:11)

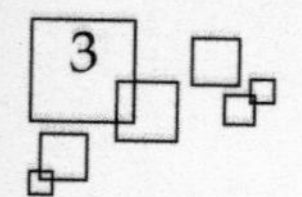

"Mountaintop experiences" are what we call life-changing, significant experiences in our lives. For some people in the Bible, that was literally true—they had significant experiences on top of real mountains. For example, Moses on Mount Sinai, Abraham on Mount Moriah, and Elijah on Mount Carmel. In the letter box below find the names of mountains mentioned in the Bible.

M	N	O	G	I	L	E	A	D	S	P	O	W	N
T	A	R	A	R	A	N	X	P	E	R	Q	N	M
O	H	R	S	A	P	O	M	N	I	Q	D	C	I
N	S	O	A	Q	M	M	B	N	R	O	H	B	Z
C	A	R	M	E	L	R	D	L	P	A	Q	W	I
Z	B	O	I	B	R	E	U	S	I	Q	P	P	R
I	X	G	A	A	S	H	O	R	P	G	X	I	E
O	P	Q	N	L	P	Z	O	L	I	V	E	S	G
N	E	B	O	Q	P	M	P	B	N	M	G	G	A
O	N	S	T	T	A	B	O	R	P	Q	N	A	G
S	I	N	A	I	Z	T	S	N	P	G	R	H	W

Scripture Pool

GENESIS 8:4 PSALM 68:15 1 KINGS 18:19 DEUTERONOMY 27:13 JUDGES 2:9
2 SAMUEL 1:6 JOSHUA 13:11 NUMBERS 34:7 GENESIS 22:2 DEUTERONOMY 34:1
MATTHEW 24:3 NUMBERS 21:20 2 KINGS 19:31 JUDGES 4:6 GENESIS 14:5–6
EXODUS 19:11 JUDGES 7:3 DEUTERONOMY 11:29

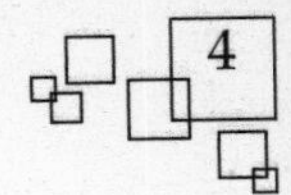

Stay in a humble frame of mind to decipher this one.

Clue: MESSIAH *is* EBFFJCA

U K B F F B V   C L B

M A B   E B B X,   T R L

M A B P   F A C K K

J Y A B L J M   M A B

B C L M A.

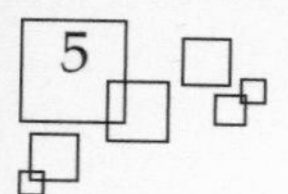

Words to the would-be wise!

Across

1 "A ____ turns away wrath" (2 words) (Proverbs 15:1)

5 "A ____ does not love one who corrects him" (Proverbs 15:12)

10 "Fools despise ____ and instruction" (Proverbs 1:7)

12 "Train ____ a child in the way he should go" (Proverbs 22:6)

13 A virtuous wife is worth "far above ____" (Proverbs 31:10)

14 "Like one who takes away a garment in ____ weather . . . is one who sings songs to a heavy heart" (Proverbs 25:20)

17 Proverbs of ____

19 "____ is a little with the fear of Lord, than great treasure with trouble" (Proverbs 15:16)

21 "Let your eyes ____ straight ahead" (Proverbs 4:25)

22 "Keep your ____ with all diligence" (Proverbs 4:23)

23 One of six things the Lord hates: "a ____ look" (Proverbs 6:17)

24 "____ in the Lord with all your heart" (Proverbs 3:5)

26 "It is easier for a ____ [pl.] to go through the eye of a needle than for rich man to enter the kingdom of God" (Matthew 19:24)

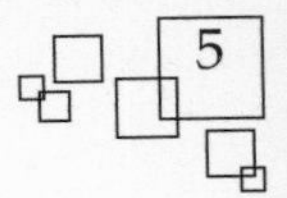

28 "Like one who binds ____ in a sling is he who gives honor to a fool" (2 words) (Proverbs 26:8)

31 "For the commandment is a lamp, and the law a ____" (Proverbs 6:23)

33 "____ for the upright, the establishes his way" (Proverbs 21:29)

34 "Do not ____ the bread of a miser" (Proverbs 23:6)

35 Three too-wonderful things: "the way of a ____ on a rock" (Proverbs 30:18–19)

37 "The ____ of the righteous is choice silver" (Proverbs 10:20)

40 "Let her own works ____ her in the gates" (Proverbs 31:31)

42 "For the ____ gives wisdom" (Proverbs 2:6)

44 Riches sometimes "fly away like an ____" (Proverbs 23:5)

46 "The LORD is the maker of them ____" (Proverbs 22:2)

47 "____ who go to her [evil] return" (Proverbs 2:19)

Down

1 "As iron sharpens iron, ____ a man sharpens the countenance of his friend" (Proverbs 27:17)

2 "Go ____ the ant, you sluggard!" (Proverbs 6:6)

3 Worthless persons . . . "____ [pl.] discord" (Proverbs 6:12, 14)

4 "He who spares his ____ hates his son" (Proverbs 13:24)

6 "A ____ rages and is self-confident" (Proverbs 14:16)

7 "He that regardeth ____ is prudent" (Proverbs 15:5, KJV)

8 "By me [wisdom] princes ____" (Proverbs 8:16)

9 Proof of payment made

11 "Fools despise wisdom and ____" (Proverbs 1:7)

14 "Do not despise the chastening of the LORD, nor detest His ____" (Proverbs 3:11)

15 "He who rolls a stone will have it roll back ____ him" (Proverbs 26:27)

16 "The hand of the ____ makes rich" (Proverbs 10:4)

18 "Where no ____ are, the trough is clean" (Proverbs 14:4)

19 "Earnestly desire the ____ gifts" (1 Corinthians 12:31)

20 "The ____ of the wicked are an abomination to the LORD" (Proverbs 15:26)

25 "The desire of the righteous is ____ good" (Proverbs 11:23)

27 "He who has a ____ hand becomes poor" (Proverbs 10:4)

29 "Will you ____ your eyes on that which is not?" (Proverbs 23:5)

30 "Wisdom . . . speaks her ____" (Proverbs 1:20–21)

32 "Seldom set foot in your neighbor's ____" (Proverbs 25:17)

36 "Ask . . . the birds of the air, and they will ____ you" (Job 12:7)

37 "Wise men ____ away wrath" (Proverbs 29:8)

38 To fail to heed God's proverbs

39 "Do not ____ your heart be glad when he [your enemy] stumbles" (Proverbs 24:17)

41 "Deceit is ____ the heart of those who devise evil" (Proverbs 12:20)

43 "____ you see a man hasty in his words? There is more hope for a fool than for him" (Proverbs 29:20)

45 "Do not ____ hastily to court" (Proverbs 25:8)

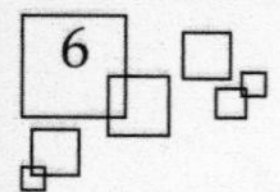

*U*nscramble the words below and then fit them into the grid. You'll reveal the name of the person to whom all these words are related!

HEAGI	IUPRM	EFSSAT
NEAUBQT	MAHAN	LAOGLSW
TVSAHI	HNSUSAH	HEZRES
MEDOARCI		AHSAURESU

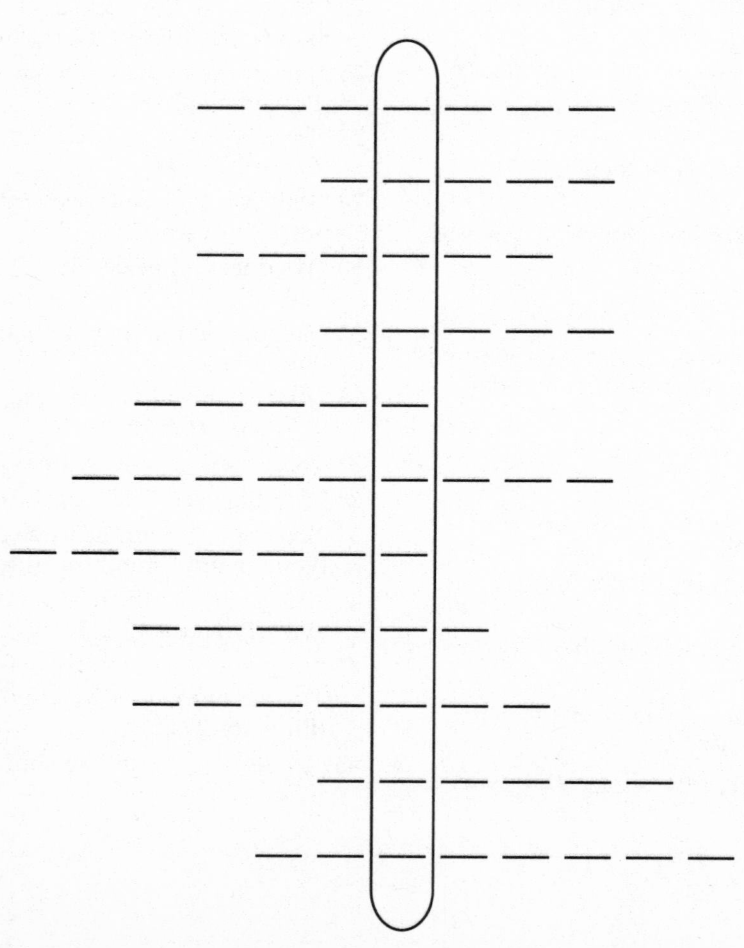

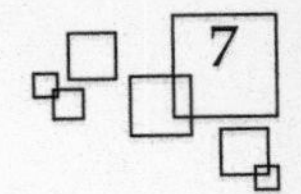

Life might not seem fair, but God is just. He has shown us the way to eternal life . . . and leaves the decision making to us. The twenty-two words hidden in this puzzle are taken from the well-known story of Lazarus and the rich man in Luke 16, which illustrates the point.

I A T F L G C O N A D F P O S E W H
R O Y S T M N F R A G G E B U S I R
T E C T H O T E E I R N E T A G F M
O G R E M E N L N S A C L R D O C G
L R E H D K B G T I R G E I S D R E
A S M P B A J N U E L L P C U W U S
C G O O T V E H T E P H F H R S M Q
U U I R D P I A B R A H A M A O B B
K L D P E L W N U D H B K A Z J S T
H F A R J S V P E S L E G N A V L W
B S E S O M W S M B C L P U L N K A
U E D V D P D J D E D A U S R E P C
R E L A C R O S N T U S R U P A K O

Word Pool

MERCY SORES GULF DEAD MOSES TABLE
REPENT TONGUE LINEN WATER ABRAHAM PURPLE HADES ANGELS
PERSUADED RICH MAN LAZARUS DOGS CRUMBS GATE BEGGAR PROPHETS

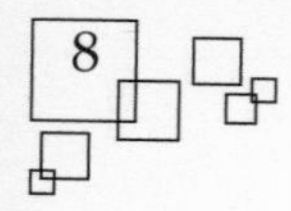

Giant vs. Shepherd

The young shepherd David was dwarfed by the Philistine giant Goliath who stood six cubits and a span (over nine feet tall). Heavily armed, Goliath jeered his enemy's choice of David to battle with him in a showdown between Philistia and Israel in the valley of Elah.

It wasn't exactly that David was the Israelites' choice, it was more that David was the only willing volunteer. In fact, David was insulted at Goliath's challenge, and he asked, "Who is this uncircumcised Philistine, that he should defy the armies of the living God?" (1 Samuel 17:26).

What were David's fighting credentials? He told King Saul that he had slain a lion and a bear when they came after his flock of sheep. "This uncircumcised Philistine will be like one of them," (v. 36) he told Saul, convincing the king to let him go to battle for the army of Israel.

Besides having the tactical advantage of the long-range slingshot, David claimed the Lord gave him another advantage: "The LORD does not save with sword and spear; for the battle is the LORD's" (v. 47). After the stone flew out of David's sling, knocking Goliath to the ground, David ran over to the Philistine, drew Goliath's sword from its sheath, and cut off the giant's head.

Help David gather five stones for his battle against Goliath. Do not cross over a path that has already been used.

Start →

End

*F*ind your way to the foot of the cross!

Start

End

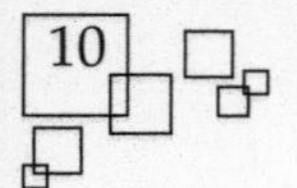

*Y*our spirit doesn't need to diet.

Clue: MESSIAH *is* CWAAZIP

M O W A A W Q   L T W   G P U A W

K P U   P S E N W T   L E Q

G P Z T A G   Y U T

T Z N P G W U S A E W A A,

Y U T   G P W J   A P L O O

M W   Y Z O O W Q.

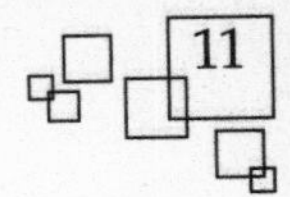

*A*ge is not a factor when it comes to God's kingdom. He is able to use all of us, no matter how young or old we are. This puzzle will given you a glimpse of how God's Word views age.

Across

3 God will carry this "house" till it's old (Isaiah 46:3–4)

6 Young men will see these (Acts 2:17)

7 Renew my youth, like this bird's (Psalm 103:5)

9 As a young man, you "took steps" where you wished (John 21:18)

11 These "good people" will still bear a harvest in old age (Psalm 92:12–14)

13 In Esther, the letter to these "cities" said kill all Jews, young and old (Esther 3:13)

15 An old wineskin might need one (Matthew 9:16–17)

17 Remember God in your youth, before "hard" days come (Ecclesiastes 12:1)

19 As a young man, you also "equipped" yourself (John 21:18)

22 Exalt your youth: be an example of "wholesomeness" (1 Timothy 4:12)

23 Don't despise this woman when she's old (Proverbs 23:22)

24 The glory of young men is their "power" (Proverbs 20:29)

25 Old men shall have this (sing.) while they are asleep (Acts 2:17)

Down

1 David: Don't remember the "follies" (sing.) of my youth (Psalm 25:7)

2 Better is a wise youth than a "silly" old king who won't listen (Ecclesiastes 4:13)

3 His book prophesied #6 and #25 Across (Joel 2:28)

4 Now old, David hadn't seen good people "beseeching" for bread (Psalm 37:25)

5 These "seniors" were first to die near Ezekiel's temple (Ezekiel 9:6)

8 Purge old leaven; be a new "chunk" (1 Corinthians 5:7)

10 The "posterity" of #4 Down

11 In a sound church, older women's behavior is "devout" (Titus 2:3)

12 Timothy's "essence" was to be an example to believers (1 Timothy 4:12)

14 From their youth, Israel and Judah did "iniquity" before God (Jeremiah 32:30)

16 God was the psalmist's "belief" from his youth (Psalm 71:5)

18 The "harvest" of #11 Across

20 Because of his youth, he was afraid to offer Job advice (Job 32:6)

21 The old lion perishes for lack of "foood" (Job 4:11)

23 The young and old were slain in Ezekiel, but not those who bore this "label" (Ezekiel 9:6)

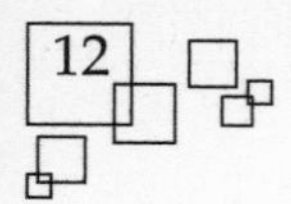

God's promise seemed almost beyond belief—but it proved true.

Clue: **MESSIAH** *is* **NHLLXRG**

X BXWW NRFH JVT R

PUHRC ERCXVE; X BXWW

IWHLL JVT REQ NRFH

JVTU ERNH PUHRC; REQ

JVT LGRWW IH R IWHLLXEP.

X BXWW IWHLL CGVLH BGV

IWHLL JVT, REQ X BXWW

ZTULH GXN BGV ZTULHL

JVT; REQ XE JVT RWW CGH

YRNXWXHL VY CGH HRUCG

LGRWW IH IWHLLHQ.

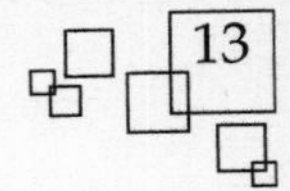

"Behold, a sower went out to sow...." Jesus taught about the kingdom of heaven by using parables. Fill in the clues from answers found in Matthew 13:3–23, to find the yield of good soil.

1. Example of one who sowed
2. Without roots, a person can easily "fall or trip"
3. Seed sown by the wayside can be easily "devoured" (2 words)
4. The birds in the parable (2 words)
5. Thorns
6. The soil or ground
7. Stony soil lacked this
8. The "crop" or harvest
9. The deceitfulness of riches can do this to the Word
10. Scorched by the sun
11. Seed (3 words)

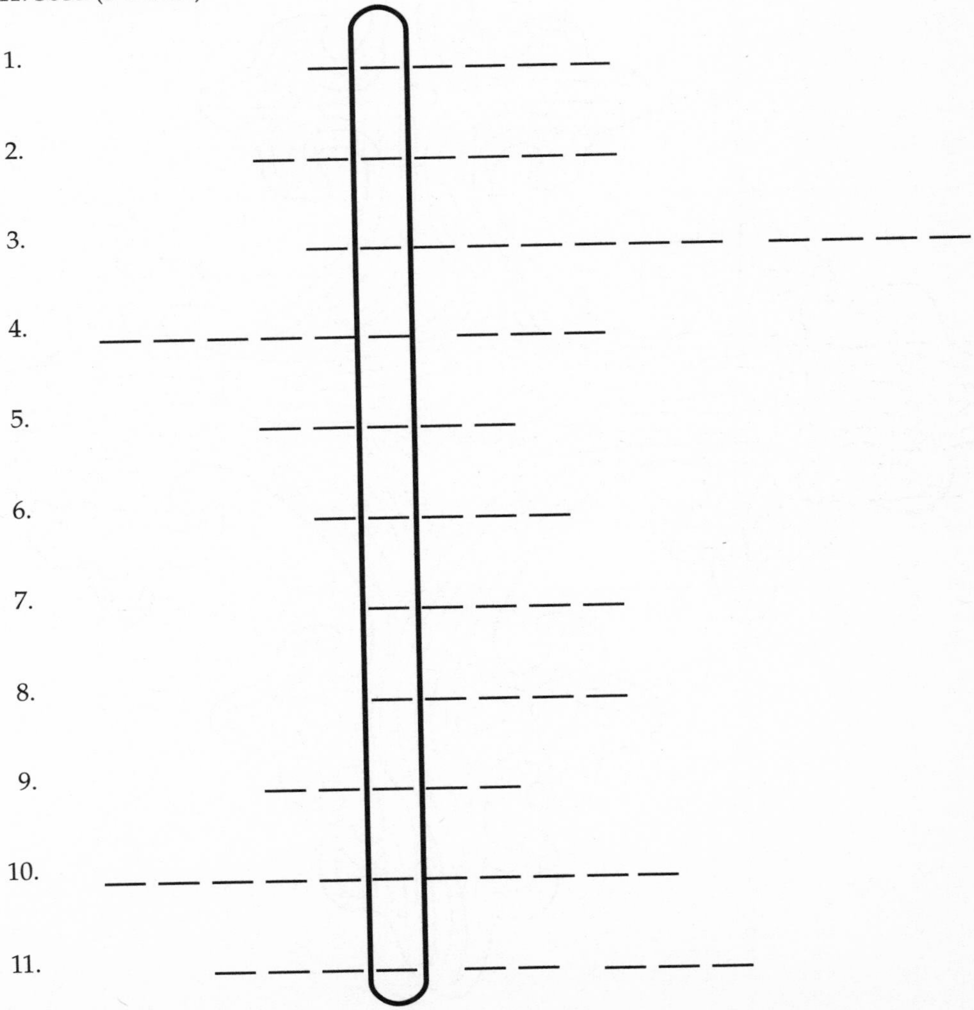

1. _ _ _ _ _ _

2. _ _ _ _ _ _ _

3. _ _ _ _ _ _ _ _ _ _ _ _ _

4. _ _ _ _ _ _ _ _ _

5. _ _ _ _ _

6. _ _ _ _ _

7. _ _ _ _ _

8. _ _ _ _ _

9. _ _ _ _ _

10. _ _ _ _ _ _ _ _ _ _ _

11. _ _ _ _ _ _ _ _ _

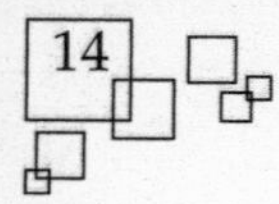

The Trinity Cross

The Trinity Cross—which honors the Father, Son, and Holy Spirit—is one of the most beautiful and elaborate of all cross designs. It is based on a double three-fold design—three of the three-petal fleur-de-lis designs on each arm of the cross.

This cross is one of a number of three-fold designs that are of Greek origin. The cross is frequently used as a church emblem on embroidered items that are hung or worn during the Trinity season of the liturgical church calendar.

Start →

← End

*U*nscramble the words below and then place them in the grid. We've given you their common denominator as a starting point!

RHTIINGB
FENSOSCINO
NOITAERC
ENSEVSIGORF
OJY
ECNEPREATN
UMSINSBISO

CGLNEIASN
CIVNOCNOIT
TAHIF
EMODEFR
LANEEWR
NIAOSRTRTOE
ONNUI

_ R _ _ _ _ _

_ _ _ _ _ _ E _ _ _ _

C _ _ _ _ _ _ _ _ _

_ _ _ _ O _ _ _ _ _ _

_ _ N _ _ _ _ _ _ _

C _ _ _ _ _ _ _

_ I _ _ _ _ _ _

_ L _ _ _ _ _ _ _

_ _ I _ _

_ _ _ _ _ A _

_ _ _ _ _ T _ _ _ _

_ _ _ _ _ I _ _ _ _ _

_ O _

_ N _ _ _

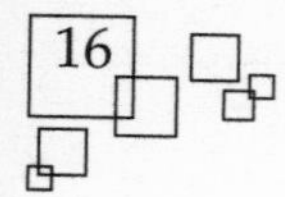

Take His Easy Yoke

Jesus said, "Take My yoke upon you and learn from Me, for I am gentle and lowly in heart, and you will find rest for your souls. For My yoke is easy and My burden is light" (Matthew 11:29–30).

Find your way through this maze by creating a string of *E*s.

	E	E	E	E	E	E	E	E	E	E	E	E	E	E	E	E	E	E	E	E	E	E	E	E	E	E	E	E	E	R	X	B	H	W	S	R	H	F	G
	E	R	F	E	W	F	X	D	Y	D	R	U	H	R	F	H	K	D	B	U	K	N	Z	F	P	E	E	E	E	E	E	E	E	E	E	E	E	E	H
	E	Y	G	F	X	N	H	P	P	S	F	Z	L	G	E	E	E	E	E	E	E	E	E	E	D	G	P	O	B	F	B	S	F	H	N	F	S	E	F
	E	I	F	E	E	E	E	E	E	E	E	E	E	E	H	B	F	H	F	W	W	K	M	B	E	E	E	E	E	E	E	E	E	E	E	E	P	F	H
Start →	E	E	E	F	O	S	F	F	H	G	K	K	P	H	K	E	E	E	E	T	U	Y	R	F	F	H	W	P	F	B	D	T	F	A	M	H	E	E	E
	F	W	F	D	P	H	E	E	E	K	R	L	B	C	D	P	G	E	E	E	E	R	T	K	H	G	Q	L	E	E	E	V	N	P	G	B	H	F	E
End →	E	E	E	E	L	K	E	F	K	E	E	E	E	E	E	E	K	M	F	F	P	E	U	E	E	E	E	K	E	R	E	E	E	E	E	E	E	E	E
	E	S	F	E	V	U	E	G	P	E	F	P	E	K	H	F	E	C	H	J	K	F	E	M	E	P	E	N	E	H	W	M	B	E	P	E	P	F	P
	S	E	J	E	A	L	E	H	D	E	H	R	E	P	P	H	F	E	K	P	J	E	P	P	E	K	E	F	E	D	S	C	E	E	F	E	K	H	K
	J	E	O	E	Z	P	E	S	R	E	D	N	E	D	R	R	N	P	E	E	E	P	T	D	E	M	E	G	E	S	B	E	N	E	U	E	J	K	M
	Y	E	P	E	F	M	E	N	F	E	B	U	E	R	N	E	P	O	F	E	M	J	N	B	E	B	E	H	B	F	E	S	P	E	K	E	U	B	N
	I	E	D	E	H	N	E	V	B	K	H	L	E	T	Y	E	L	X	H	E	C	H	V	J	E	F	E	T	F	E	P	P	H	E	L	E	Y	E	H
	N	E	B	E	K	A	E	E	E	E	K	D	E	Y	T	E	T	M	P	E	G	B	F	E	E	G	E	S	E	F	G	R	R	E	N	E	T	E	R
	V	E	W	E	L	C	F	B	H	E	M	N	E	M	E	E	X	G	N	E	R	R	E	H	L	H	E	D	G	P	E	E	E	E	B	E	R	E	G
	C	E	F	E	F	X	G	E	E	E	O	T	E	E	C	N	N	R	S	E	T	E	B	D	P	D	E	Z	B	D	E	Q	B	P	D	E	F	E	H
	S	E	Y	F	E	Z	H	F	B	F	A	E	G	N	L	E	E	E	E	E	Y	E	E	E	F	S	P	E	H	R	D	C	C	L	E	F	E	H	F
	T	E	H	E	S	E	K	L	K	P	E	N	H	P	M	E	P	F	K	F	U	F	H	E	G	N	T	F	E	S	B	V	R	E	S	F	E	E	D
	E	E	N	E	F	F	E	E	E	E	F	R	K	R	V	E	M	H	F	E	E	E	E	E	E	E	E	G	P	E	E	E	E	H	P	E	C	E	C
	E	F	V	E	U	G	W	F	K	G	H	U	S	K	R	K	F	K	G	F	K	F	N	W	H	O	M	H	N	E	T	Z	Y	C	L	E	X	E	S
	E	T	Z	E	O	V	H	S	H	K	E	E	E	E	E	E	E	E	E	E	E	E	E	E	E	U	V	J	R	E	N	U	P	H	K	E	S	E	X
	E	N	W	E	X	B	L	R	D	D	H	F	B	H	W	F	H	F	N	F	J	F	D	P	E	T	E	E	E	E	E	E	E	E	M	E	A	E	A
	E	V	F	E	E	E	E	E	E	E	E	E	E	E	E	E	B	H	P	E	K	B	B	B	E	V	F	F	P	E	M	P	F	F	N	E	W	E	D
	E	D	Y	E	R	F	Y	F	H	B	F	F	P	B	Q	M	F	K	R	E	S	H	H	F	E	W	H	X	N	K	G	H	H	P	D	E	T	E	G
	E	R	E	E	N	E	E	E	E	E	E	E	K	F	E	Y	E	P	D	E	E	E	E	E	E	E	E	E	E	E	E	E	E	E	E	E	M	E	H
	E	K	F	T	X	E	W	T	N	H	F	E	D	H	E	R	E	R	S	F	P	R	D	R	H	F	R	K	M	N	X	F	K	R	F	F	C	E	K
	E	E	E	E	E	E	P	N	E	K	H	E	F	N	E	T	E	Y	Z	P	T	K	P	F	P	G	P	F	Y	D	G	B	D	B	P	P	X	E	M
	F	L	F	F	Q	F	C	B	E	D	B	E	K	C	E	P	E	E	E	E	E	E	E	E	E	E	E	E	E	E	E	E	E	E	E	E	E	E	V
	H	C	L	U	T	S	E	C	E	R	E	E	E	E	E	S	H	N	F	V	H	F	G	H	F	H	F	R	N	F	R	N	G	F	S	S	P	E	B
	F	E	E	E	E	E	E	D	E	E	K	F	P	E	F	C	K	H	Y	B	E	E	E	E	E	E	H	F	B	E	E	E	E	E	E	N	K	E	C
	E	M	F	E	N	W	F	F	E	E	P	H	D	E	E	E	E	E	E	E	E	B	K	K	H	K	E	H	H	E	H	C	H	F	D	T	D	E	P
	E	Z	R	E	C	K	E	E	J	E	D	M	H	E	F	C	B	H	F	S	E	E	E	E	E	K	G	E	E	E	E	E	E	E	E	E	B	E	R
	E	F	Z	E	E	E	F	H	K	E	N	V	K	E	H	F	K	P	K	P	F	X	L	X	M	F	P	F	D	F	B	M	Y	F	P	E	R	E	U
	E	B	A	P	S	U	P	L	E	E	S	B	L	E	E	E	E	E	E	E	E	E	E	E	E	E	E	E	E	E	E	T	P	N	U	E	Y	E	S

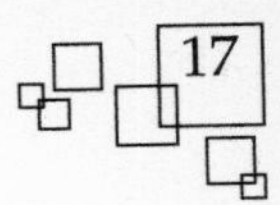

*B*y adding, subtracting, multiplying, and dividing the numbers found in the Gospel accounts of Jesus' miracles, you will arrive at the number of persons Jesus sent out to preach, teach, and heal in His name.

The number of men who were fed with the miracle multiplication of the boy's lunch of loaves and fish (John 6:10)		_____
Divided by . . . The number of lepers who were cleansed and healed by Jesus (Luke 17:12–14)	÷	_____
Multiplied by . . . The number of days Jesus was in the tomb before His resurrection (Luke 24:7)	×	_____
Divided by . . . The number of years the woman suffered with the issue of blood before she was healed (Matthew 9:20)	÷	_____
Plus . . . The number of years the lame man laid by the pool of Bethesda (John 5:5)	+	_____
Minus . . . The number of waterpots filled with water that Jesus turned into wine (John 2:6–9)	−	_____
Plus . . . The number of friends who carried the paralytic man to Jesus to be healed (Mark 2:3)	+	_____
Minus . . . The number of sons of the widow woman who had a son who was raised from the dead (Luke 7:12)	−	_____
Divided by . . . The number of days Lazarus was in the tomb (John 11:39)	÷	_____
Minus . . . The number of demons cast out of Mary Magdalene (Luke 8:2)	−	_____
Plus . . . The number of blind men who received their sight as Jesus passed by (Matthew 20:30)	+	_____
Multiplied by . . . The number of men from the country of the Gergesenes who were delivered of demons (Matthew 8:28)	×	_____
Equals . . . The number of followers Jesus sent out two by two to minister in His name (Luke 10:1)	=	_____

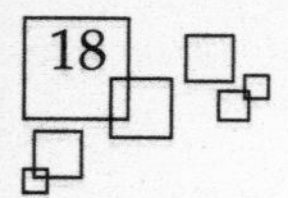

*F*aith in God can move mountains. Just ask the people who are singled out in Hebrews 11.

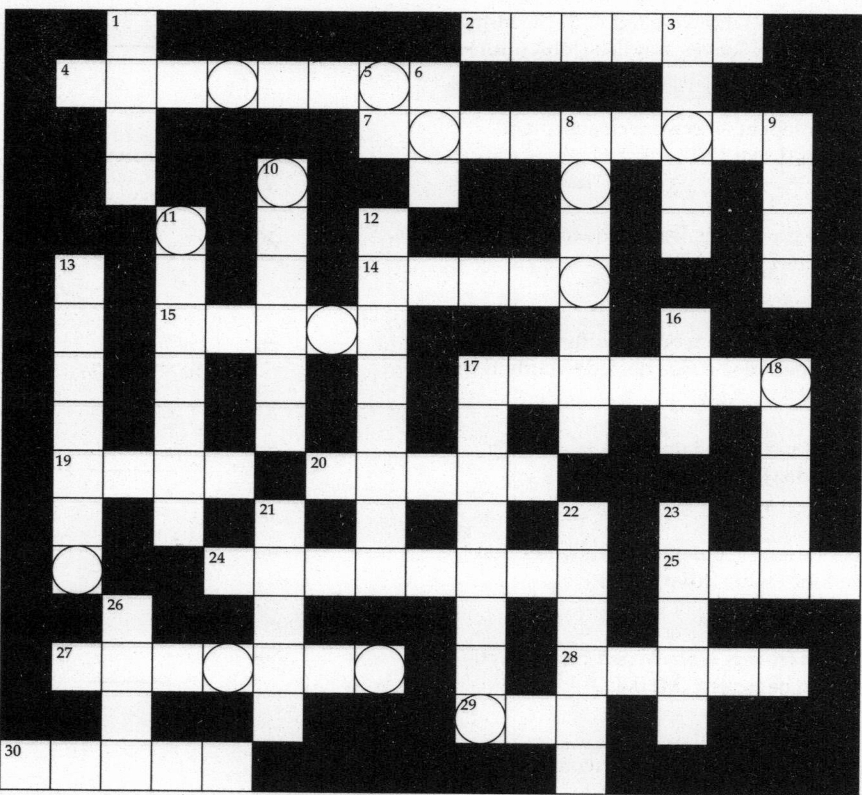

Across

2 Hannah offered him to the Lord before he was born

4 God's faithful servants subdued these "realms"

7 Cain's brother offered a better sacrifice, proving he was "virtuous"

14 Moses passed up the treasures of this country and instead chose the reproach of Christ

15 Some of the faithful wandered about in skins made from this animal

17 The faithful shall be made "without blemish" along with those faithful ones who came after them

19 Abraham was waiting for the "large town" whose builder and maker is God

20 When he was dying, he blessed each of the sons of Joseph

24 This Gileadite, though the son of a harlot, was a mighty man of valor; he defeated the Ammonites

25 By faith he offered a "more excellent sacrifice"

27 By faith, Abraham lived in Canaan as in a foreign "land"

28 He was the son Sarah prayed for

29 Moses refused to be called the "male child" of Pharaoh's daughter

30 This harlot received the spies from Israel with peace, and her life was spared

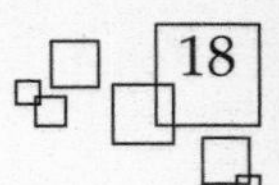

Down

1 Daniel was one who stopped the mouth of this wild animal

3 Because he was "taken away," he did not see death

5 Mister (abbr.)

6 Moses chose to suffer with God's people rather than enjoy the passing pleasures of "wrongdoing"

8 Some of the faithful endured this and refused deliverance, so as to obtain a better resurrection

9 From Abraham came descendants as innumerable as grains of this substance

10 The valiant faithful caused the armies of these "foreigners" to flee

11 The Sahara is an example of these places where the faithful wandered

12 The "censure" of Christ was more attractive to Moses than money

13 Faith caused the walls of this city to fall

16 This sea retreated at the advance of the Israelites

17 Jeremiah was one of these (pl.)

18 How many months Moses was hidden by his parents before being set afloat

21 Abraham and his family lived in these portable homes

22 Paul's and Silas's were loosed, and a jailer was converted

23 With Deborah's help, he defeated Sisera's army

26 He knew the dew would drop

Bonus:
Unscramble the circled letters to tell you
what our elders in the faith obtained through faith.

__ __ __ __ __ __ __ __ __ __ __ __ __ __

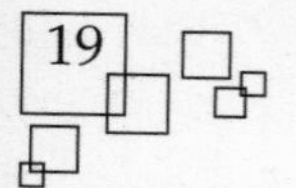

*J*esus spoke these words from a mountain.

Clue: MESSIAH *is* TWQQBYI

Z C W Q Q W A   Y F W

P I W   T W F X B J E C,

J S F   P I W N   Q I Y C C

S Z P Y B G   T W F X N.

*R*ELUCTANT *P*ROPHET

*W*hen he had time to think about it in the belly of the large fish, Jonah had a change of heart. Perhaps going to Nineveh wasn't as bad as the predicament he found himself in now. Jonah cried out to God, and God heard his prayer and delivered him from the insides of that great sea animal.

The Lord gave Jonah another chance to obey Him as He said to him again, "Arise, go to Nineveh, that great city, and preach to it the message that I tell you" (Jonah 3:2). This time, instead of fleeing from the Lord's presence, Jonah obeyed and "arose and went to Nineveh" (v. 3).

The city of Nineveh was known for its evil ways and violence (Jonah 3:8), plotting evil against the Lord (Nahum 1:11), being "full of lies" (Nahum 3:1), endless cruelty (Nahum 3:19, NIV), witchcraft and prostitution (Nahum 3:4, NIV), and exploitation (Nahum 3:16). It's no wonder Jonah was reluctant.

Jonah's decision to go to Nineveh is attributed more to his readiness to obey God than a love for the people of this wicked city. His message to the Ninevites was simple, "Yet forty days, and Nineveh shall be overthrown!" (Jonah 3:4). The Scripture says, "So the people of Nineveh believed God, proclaimed a fast, and put on sackcloth, from the greatest to the least of them" (v. 5). When God saw that they had turned from their

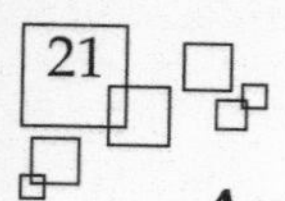

*A*ll the clues in this puzzle begin with the same leTTer!

Across

1 ____ and obey

3 Lead us not into it, we pray (Matthew 6:13)

9 Blessed is the ____ that binds our hearts in love

10 Joseph of Arimathea gave his to Jesus (Mark 15:43–46)

11 It is not for us to know these or seasons (Acts 1:7)

13 "Whatever I ____ you in the dark, speak in the light" (Matthew 10:27)

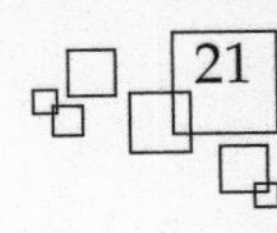

14 Where this is, there your heart is (Matthew 6:21)
15 Father, Son, and Holy Spirit
17 The Lord's fills the temple (Isaiah 6:1)
18 Doubting disciple
19 The apostle Paul left his cloak there (2 Timothy 4:13)
20 These were made of potter's clay and iron, in Daniel's vision (Daniel 2:41)
22 Judah, for example
25 ____ and fro
26 The number of men cast into Nebuchadnezzar's fiery furnace (Daniel 3:24)
28 The false shepherd will do this to the hooves of his sheep (Zechariah 11:16)
30 Saul's hometown (Acts 9:11)
31 "____ shalt not kill" (Exodus 20:13, KJV)
32 John was imprisoned on the island of Patmos for this (Revelation 1:9)
33 A place where the ram's blood was to be applied (Exodus 29:20)
36 Jesus stood ____ before the Sanhedrin, Herod, or Pilate
37 "Show me Your ways, O LORD; ____ me Your paths" (Psalm 25:4)
38 "The thorn and ____ shall grow on their altars" (Hosea 10:8)
40 "Jesus Christ is the same yesterday, ____, and forever" (Hebrews 13:8)
42 Short for trumpet
43 Where our heavenly Father sits (Revelation 3:21)
44 Jacob and Esau, for example
45 It makes us free (John 8:32)
47 Someday they will all be wiped away by God (Revelation 7:17)
48 The apostle Paul's traveling companion; he also received two letters from Paul (Acts 16:1–4)
52 We are to let our requests to God be made known with this (Philippians 4:6)
53 Jesus said the moneychangers had made the temple a den of ____ (Mark 11:17)
56 The day He arose
58 Abraham gave these to Melchizedek (Genesis 14:20)
60 The church in this city received two letters from the apostle Paul
61 We are to do this to the spirits (1 John 4:1)

Down

1 "In the world you will have ____" (John 16:33)
2 The number of days Purim is celebrated (Esther 9:26–27)
3 The one in which Moses conferred with God was named "witness" (Numbers 17:7–8)
4 He came to Jesus in the wilderness (Matthew 4:3)
5 The Lord's "eyelids ____ the sons of men" (Psalm 11:4)
6 Zacchaeus's viewing place
7 Better invested than buried (Matthew 25:15)
8 Old and New
10 Adam and Eve were told neither to eat nor ____ the fruit of the tree (Genesis 3:3)
12 Abraham was sitting here when the Lord appeared to him (Genesis 18:1)
13 ____ figuration or ____ gression
16 The wise woman makes this for herself (Proverbs 31:22)
18 Judah's were called "whiter than milk" (Genesis 49:12)
19 These appeared when the grain sprouted (Matthew 13:26)
21 The place where a poor widow gave two mites (Mark 12:41–42)
23 The way one discovers the Lord is good (Psalm 34:8)
24 Let not your heart be so (John 14:1)
27 He who sat on a white horse was called Faithful and ____ (Revelation 19:11)
29 "Do you not know that you are the ____ of God and that the Spirit of God dwells in you?" (1 Corinthians 3:16)
30 Huram came from here to do King Solomon's bronze work (1 Kings 7:13)
34 The Lord's are of peace, to give a future and a hope! (Jeremiah 29:11)
35 Every one of these will one day confess Jesus as Lord (Philippians 2:11)
36 What Jesus did when He sat down in the temple (John 8:2)
37 Jesus distributed the loaves after He had given this (John 6:11)
38 The part of Jacob's ladder that reached to heaven (Genesis 28:12)
39 The number of gerahs that make a shekel (Exodus 30:13)
41 Jesus' mock crown was made of this (John 19:5)
44 "Confidence in an unfaithful man in time of trouble is like a bad ____" (Proverbs 25:19)
46 "Touch no unclean ____" (Isaiah 52:11)
49 The Lord said, "I will send a famine on the land, not a famine of bread, nor a ____ for water, but of hearing the words of the LORD" (Amos 8:11)
50 The apostle Paul's "True son in our common faith" in Crete (Titus 1:4–5)
51 Moses appointed some to be "leaders of ____" (Deuteronomy 1:15)
54 You, in old English
55 "The LORD will make you the head and not the ____" (Deuteronomy 28:13)
57 Jesus said, "I am ____ light of the world" (John 8:12)
58 Zacchaeus and Matthew were both collectors of this
59 The number of lepers who cried to Jesus, "Master, have mercy on us!" (Luke 17:12)

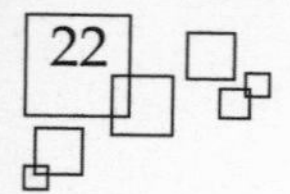

We know Him as Jesus Christ, the Son of the Living God, the Great Physician, the Author and Finisher of our faith. He is also known by a host of other names. Find as many names of Jesus as you can in this letter box.

R E A M R E S U R R E C T I O N G S
S W L E P A M O V B G D R X S J B E
C A M I V K O E F I L F O D A E R B
E N I V F D H U S I A K X D D L I H
P Z G C T E P L O R D M O F V Q D A
T S H T U R T N E S L G B N O G E I
E J T Q E D O E U H F N U Z C M G S
R B Y A T I S Q W O V T R B A I R S
K A C J R R T A B O I C E F T C O E
W I T N E S S M B R A N C H E G O M
H L N V P E A O Y A H K D R P I M D
E F O G M L D R E H P E H S D O O G
R X E G D U J G O N E W R A L M R H
A I C O R N E R S T O N E C F Y U P

Word Pool

I AM MESSIAH BRANCH PROPHET KING LAMB OF GOD JUDGE BRIDGEGROOM STAR SCEPTER CORNERSTONE LORD GOOD SHEPHERD OVERSEER ADVOCATE WITNESS LION BREAD OF LIFE DOOR RESURRECTION LIFE WAY TRUTH VINE ALMIGHTY

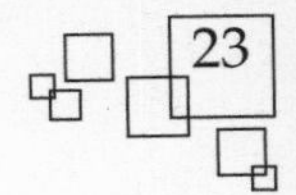

*P*salm 119 is divided into sections, each of which has been given a name. These names are provided for you below. Your challenge is to fit them into the grid! We've given you one name as a starting point.

Word Pool

ALEPH AYIN BETH DALETH GIMEL HE HETH
KAPH LAMED MEM NUN PE QOPH RESH TSADDE
SAMEK SHIN TAU TETH WAW YOD ZAYIN

*E*xcept for a few spectacular instances—a whirlwind taking Elijah to heaven and Phillip's mysterious trip to Azotus after baptizing the Ethiopian eunuch on the road to Gaza—transportation in Bible times was quite pedestrian. In the Word Pool, you'll find some of the ways that people traveled. Each of the words is hidden in the letter box below. Circle each word when you find it.

N O E P T N S Q N E R T K L J
N L O P N C K A I R P L A N E
M E S R O H P M N X L A Q Z T
O P I Y H A N X O P E N Q I O
E M N O P R O L O O B O A T W
N C A R R I A G E L O J H G E
A X A M N O S U B M A R I N E
L S A R O T M N X R A P O I T
P H O X T J K L F X O C N L W
O I M N L P T O O F E D M N Z
R P L K M N O P I S I F M N L
D K L O C A S W D O N K E Y X
Y O S K A T E S L P X A S E D
H L O R R K T E K C O R E N D

Word Pool

BOAT CAMEL CARRIAGE CART CHARIOT DONKEY FOOT
HORSE SHIP SKIFF

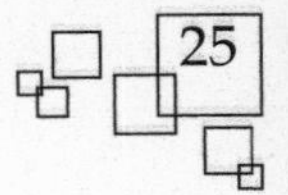

New Life

Eggs are one of the oldest, most recognized symbols of spring and fertility. For Christians, eggs are associated with Easter as a sign of new life and resurrection. In this symbolism, the shell of the Easter egg is compared to a rock tomb out of which emerges a new life.

The tradition of decorating Easter eggs is popular in many countries. Dyeing Easter eggs has been practiced since at least the fifteenth century and may have been practiced even earlier than that. In many countries eggs are dyed red to represent the shed blood of Jesus. Easter egg designs range from the elaborate Ukranian Easter eggs to the home-dyed Easter activity of many children. Decorated Easter eggs are often exchanged or given to friends and loved ones to signify the renewal of relationships.

Egg-rolling is a popular Easter event for children; the child who gets his or her egg to the finish line first without breaking it is the winner. Tradition claims that the egg roll is symbolic of the rolling away of the stone from the tomb on Easter morning.

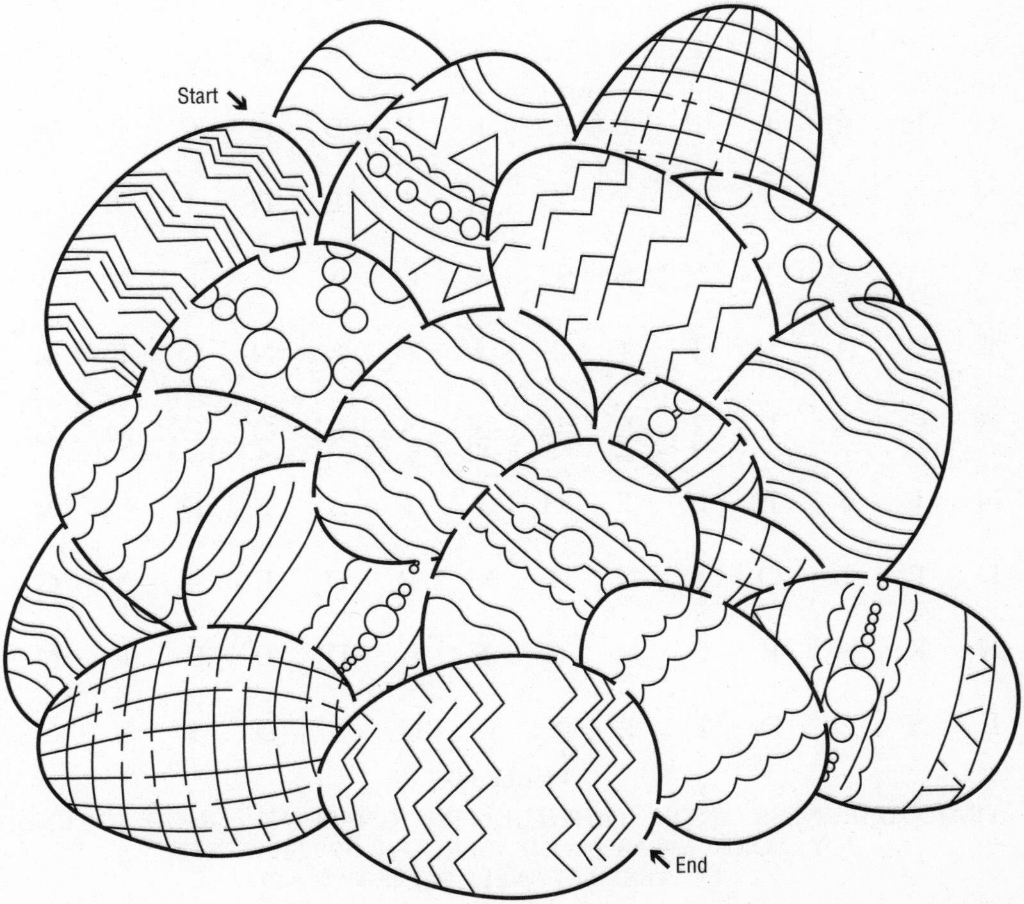

Start ↘

↖ End

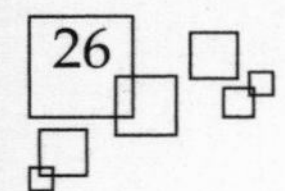

*I*n the letter box below are hidden words from the parable of the talents in Matthew 25:14–30.

U S O P G P L Y R N G P W D
W I C K E D O X N T P G I R
E N O P T J A N L R A A O N
E R A D O O G E I F R M I B
P O N U I U X N O F R E P O
I N O X P R E D A N L O N W
N T A L E N T S X S O N R J
G N O L P E U E P S H R E W
N X D F L Y O R S E H I T E
A T O I N S U V O N I E N S
E W I V J T L A R K N O E G
W O N E T R U N A R O O M G
N L I L U F H T I A F D O N
D R L O B N I M P D E A N G
N K W R O N G F A D E S E N
E N O D L L E W H S D I Y O

Word Pool

AFRAID DARKNESS ENTER FAITHFUL FIVE GNASHING GOOD JOURNEY
JOY LORD MONEY ONE SERVANT TALENTS TEN
TWO WEEPING WELL DONE WICKED

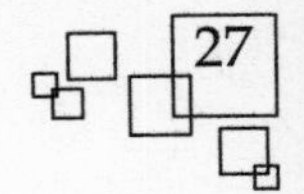

*A*rrange the events of the Exodus in correct chronological sequence, and line up the bold letters to reveal God's cry for His people.

WAT**E**R AND MANNA PROVIDED
M**O**UNT SINAI
CROSSING THE JORDAN RIV**E**R
MOS**E**S APPOINTED LEADER
PHARAOH DEFEATED
THE PR**O**MISED LAND
EGYPTIAN S**L**AVERY
FORTY YEARS IN THE WI**L**DERNESS
FREEDO**M**
PLAGUES AND DEA**T**H OF FIRSTBORN
CONQUERING CANAANITE KIN**G**S
REBELLION IN WILDERNESS OF **P**ARAN
ACROSS THE RED SEA ON DR**Y** GROUND

1. ______________________ ___ ______________________
2. ______________________ ___ ______________________
3. ______________________ ___ ______________________
4. ______________________ ___ ______________________
5. ______________________ ___ ______________________
6. ______________________ ___ ______________________
7. ______________________ ___ ______________________
8. ______________________ ___ ______________________
9. ______________________ ___ ______________________
10. ______________________ ___ ______________________
11. ______________________ ___ ______________________
12. ______________________ ___ ______________________
13. ______________________ ___ ______________________

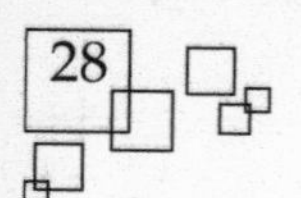

*A*s the children of Israel traveled through the wilderness on the way to the promised land, the Lord gave Moses very detailed instructions to make a tabernacle so He could be among His chosen people. The clues below are based on the construction of the portable tabernacle.

Across

1 The bread of God's presence (Exodus 25:30)

6 Reconcile, make "at one" (Exodus 30:10)

10 The mercy seat is where God said He would ____ with Moses (Exodus 25:22)

12 One of the metals given to God for the tabernacle (Exodus 25:3)

15 Each cherub had two of these (sing.) (Exodus 25:20)

18 Made from stacte, onycha, galbanum, frankincense (Exodus 30:34–35)

19 By ____ God led the children of Israel by a pillar of cloud (Exodus 13:21)

20 The fabric of the tabernacle curtains (Exodus 26:1)

21 The wood of the table of the showbread (Exodus 25:23)

22 Precious metal that covered the ark of the covenant (Exodus 25:11)

23 Offering (sing.) for the anointing oil (Exodus 25:6)

25 This substance was put in the ark of the covenant to remind the children of Israel of God's provision for them (Exodus 16:33–34)

26 God ordered the tabernacle to be built as a place for Him to ____ among the people (Exodus 25:8)

28 The outer area surrounding the tabernacle; it measured one hundred by fifty cubits (Exodus 27:9)

29 Neuter pronoun
33 Oil made from this was burned for light (Exodus 27:20)
34 The people brought "____ rings and nose rings, rings and necklaces, all jewelry of gold" to offer to the Lord (Exodus 35:22)
35 The robe of the ephod was of this color (Exodus 28:31)
37 Color of thread other than gold, blue, and scarlet (Exodus 39:2)
38 ____ rings were set in the ____ corners of the ark so it could be carried (Exodus 37:3)
41 Made of stone, these contained God's law and were put in the ark of the covenant (Deuteronomy 10:5)
43 Pomegranates decorated the ____ of the priest's robe (Exodus 39:24)
44 The south and north sides of the court of the tabernacle were each ____ hundred cubits long (Exodus 27:9, 11)
45 The most sacred furnishing in the tabernacle; it was to remind the children of Israel of God's presence with them (Exodus 25:10)
46 Three bowls of the lampstand were fashioned like blossoms from this tree (Exodus 25:33)
49 God gave this leader His instructions to build the tabernacle (Exodus 25:1)
55 Candlestick (Exodus 25:31)
57 The part of the tabernacle behind the second veil, the Holiest of ____ (Hebrews 9:3)
58 These (sing.) were connected with clasps to couple the curtains together (Exodus 26:5)
60 The first hight priest of Israel (Exodus 28:1)
61 Gifted and talented in design and art (Exodus 31:4)
63 Strand of fiber used for loops (Exodus 26:4)
65 The people were restrained from bringing more material because they brought ____ much (Exodus 36:7)
66 Clothing (sing.) (Exodus 39:1)
67 The court of the tabernacle was fifty cubits ____ (Exodus 27:13)
68 Consecrated, sacred place (Exodus 25:8)

Down

2 Opposite of him
3 He was filled with the Spirit of God to design works of art (Exodus 31:2–4, KJV)
4 The stones on the ephod were ____ memorial stones for the sons of Israel (Exodus 28:12)
5 The ____ seat symbolized God's throne (Exodus 25:22)
7 Garments of ministry were made of blue, purple, and scarlet ____ (Exodus 39:1)
8 All the ____ and women whose hearts were willing were to bring material for the tabernacle (Exodus 35:29)
9 The tent of meeting; dwelling place (Exodus 40:2)
11 Each board was ____ cubits long (Exodus 26:16)
12 Aaron's rod that ____ was kept in the ark of the covenant (Hebrews 9:4)
13 One of the precious stones in the vestments of the priests (Exodus 25:7)
14 Moses met with God on this mountain (Exodus 24:16)
15 The priests were commanded to ____ the ephod, breastplate, tunic, turban, trousers, and sash, plate of the holy crown to minister in the holy place
16 Burnt offering and ____ offering were offered on the same altar (Exodus 40:29)
17 The gold cherubim were at the two ____ of the mercy seat (Exodus 25:19)
24 Winged creatures (Exodus 25:22)
27 The priests were to wash at the ____ before offering burnt offerings (Exodus 30:18)
28 Unit of linear measure equal to about eighteen inches (Exodus 25:10)
30 Portable dwelling place (Exodus 36:14)
31 God's chosen nation
32 Column; these supported the hangings around the court (Exodus 38:10)
33 A gift to the Lord (Exodus 25:2)
36 A priestly upper garment (Exodus 39:2)
39 An item used by the high priest to help determine God's guidance (Exodus 28:30)
40 The number of lamps on the lampstand (Exodus 37:23)
42 The ____s of badgers and rams were used as a covering for the tabernacle (Exodus 26:14)
47 Sweet incense was burned ____ the gold altar (Exodus 40:26–27)
48 One of the precious stones of the breastplate (Exodus 28:18)
50 Made from myrrh, cinnamon, cane, cassia, and olive oil to be used for anointing (Exodus 30:23–25)
51 The Lord said He would ____ with Moses about the commands He gave to the children of Israel (Exodus 25:22)
52 God told Moses to put water ____ the laver (Exodus 40:7)
53 The veil divided the holy ____ and the Most Holy (Exodus 26:33)
54 Set apart; sanctified (Exodus 26:33)
56 To pour out or apply oil as a ritual of consecration (Exodus 29:7)
57 There were two of these (sing.) in the tabernacle—one for burnt offerings and one for incense (Exodus 37:25; 38:1)
59 The ____ of the Lord filled the tabernacle (Exodus 40:34)
62 God told Moses, "No man shall ____ Me, and live" (Exodus 33:20)
64 The laver was set between the tabernacle ____ the altar (Exodus 40:30)

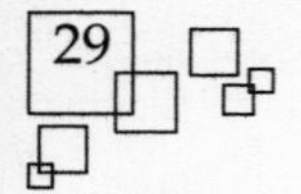

*S*ometimes starting at the bottom and working your way to the top is the key to finding truth. String together the letters in the box below to read one of the most famous statements made by Jesus in the New Testament.

E	N	A	E	E	Y	M
E	D	H	D	D	W	N
R	T	T	A	N	O	I
F	H	U	N	I	R	E
U	E	R	D	S	D	D
O	T	T	Y	E	Y	I
Y	R	E	O	L	O	B
E	U	H	U	P	U	A
K	T	T	S	I	A	U
A	H	W	H	C	R	O
M	S	O	A	S	E	Y
L	H	N	L	I	M	F
L	A	K	L	D	Y	I

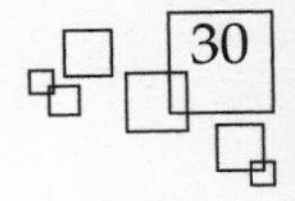

O CHRISTMAS TREE!

For most people who celebrate Christmas, a beautifully decorated Christmas tree is the center of festivities. Early Christmas tree decorations were simple, with strings of popcorn and cranberries, handmade paper ornaments, candy canes, apples, candies, cookies, and sweets. Candles added light to brighten the tree. Over the years, Christmas tree trimmings became increasingly ornate. Candles have been replaced by strings of electric lights, and the homemade ornaments have been replaced with tinsel and bright, glittering manufactured decorations.

The decoration of evergreen trees predates the use of the Christmas tree in Christian celebration. Primitive peoples believed that trees that remained green throughout winter months had special powers. The evergreen trees were used in ritual ceremonies and brought into homes to ensure the return of green vegetation.

Gradually, the decorated evergreen tree took its place in Christmas celebrations. In the fifteenth century the evergreen trees were used in German mystery plays depicting the stories of the Bible to teach Scripture. By the 1800s Christmas trees were used in the United States, brought to the U.S. by German immigrants.

Start

← End

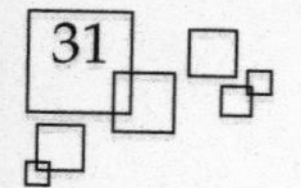

*S*ometimes it is difficult in the twilight to tell when day ends and night begins. Find the verse hidden in the box of letters below (including reference).

I D M A U Y S T

T H W E O N R I

K G T H H T E I

W S O C R O K M

S I O N F G H W

I H M E W N H N

O O S O E N N E

T C M A E N W W

H O I R L K E J

I O T H I N S 9:4

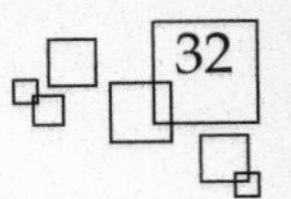

Complete the acrostic below that reveals how the Lord took care of His people as they wandered in the wilderness on the way to the promised land. Refer to Exodus 13:21; 15:22—17:16; 19:2, and Numbers 10; 12; 21.

1. It came from a rock
2. Name of place with twelve wells and seventy palm trees
3. The-Lord-Is-My-Banner was the name of the one Moses built after the victory at Rephidim
4. The way the Lord led the people by day
5. What Moses cast into the bitter waters to make them sweet
6. Place of bitter waters
7. The bread given by the Lord
8. When Moses held up his hand, the Israelites prevailed against them
9. Place where God gave the covenant
10. Name of wilderness between Elim and Sinai
11. What Moses did to reverse Miriam's leprosy
12. Amount of manna allotted per person
13. A fiery serpent was made of this and set on a pole
14. Signal announced by two silver trumpets
15. Place where Moses struck a rock and water rushed forth
16. Victory over them was marked by the defeat of king Og at Edrel
17. Type of bird that came in droves at evening to cover the camp
18. First place where water came from a rock
19. Place where the cloud settled after Sinai

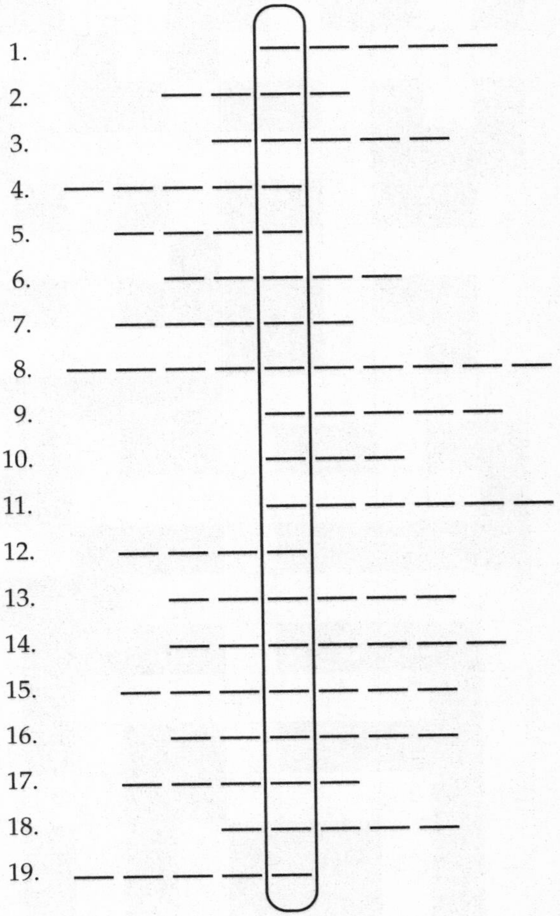

1. _ | _ | _ _ _ _
2. _ _ | _ | _
3. _ | _ | _ _ _
4. _ _ _ _ | _ |
5. _ _ _ | _ |
6. _ _ | _ | _ _
7. _ _ _ | _ | _
8. _ _ _ _ | _ | _ _ _ _ _
9. | _ | _ _ _ _
10. | _ | _ _
11. | _ | _ _ _ _ _
12. _ _ _ | _ |
13. _ _ | _ | _ _ _
14. _ _ | _ | _ _ _ _
15. _ _ _ | _ | _ _ _
16. _ _ | _ | _ _ _
17. _ _ _ | _ | _
18. _ | _ | _ _ _
19. _ _ _ _ | _ |

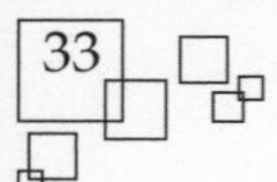

Satan tempted Eve to become like God. She believed the tempter intead of God. The clues below all have to do with the Fall.

Across

1 The angels at the east of the garden guarded the ____ to the tree of life (Genesis 3:24)

3 Adam and Eve's first home (Genesis 2:15)

5 God made this for Adam and Eve to wear after they sinned (Genesis 3:21)

8 "She ____ of its fruit and ate" (Genesis 3:6)

10 "The man has become like one ____ Us" (Genesis 3:22)

11 This place was paradise for the first man and woman (Genesis 2:8)

13 The forbidden ____ (Genesis 3:2–3)

15 Trouble and sadness increased because of Eve's sin (Genesis 3:16)

17 Crafty; the serpent was more than most (Genesis 3:1)

22 Moral purity, virtue (Genesis 3:5)

24 Ill will; hostility (Genesis 3:15)

25 #5 Across was made of this (Genesis 3:21)

27 Fearful (Genesis 3:10)

28 "And ____ ate" (Genesis 3:6)

29 Sin brought this (Romans 5:16)

30 Gave attention to (Genesis 3:17)

35 To become aware (Genesis 3:5)

37 The serpent was cursed: "On your belly you shall ____" (Genesis 3:14)

38 Pleasing, agreeable; the tree of life was ____ to look at (Genesis 3:6)

39 Disobedience, wrongdoing; missing the mark (Romans 5:12)

42 Offspring (Genesis 3:16)

43 Because of their sin, Adam and Eve were denied access to this tree (3 words), and death entered the world (Genesis 3:24)

45 Adam to Eve (Genesis 3:6)

47 Necessary for sight (Genesis 3:7)

49 God said to the woman, "What is this you have ____?" (Genesis 3:13)

50 When Adam and Eve heard this, they went and hid (Genesis 3:8)

52 Middle (Genesis 3:3)

54 The serpent lied to Eve and told her, "You will not surely ____" (Genesis 3:4)

55 Weeds that grew after the Fall (Genesis 3:18)

56 "All the ____ of your life" (Genesis 3:14)

57 Suffering; this would accompany childbearing (Genesis 3:16)

Down

2 "In ____ all die" (1 Corinthians 15:22)

3 "Mother of all living" (Genesis 3:20)

4 Neither, ____ (Genesis 3:3)

5 Come in contact with (Genesis 3:3)

6 "You shall ____ eat of it" (Genesis 3:17)

7 Damned (Genesis 3:14)

8 "The woman whom You gave ____ be with me" (Genesis 3:12)

9 Perceived, understood (Genesis 3:7)

12 Beguiled (Genesis 3:13)

13 ____ leaves were the first clothing (Genesis 3:7)

14 "Through ____ man sin entered the world" (Romans 5:12)

16 "Till you ____ to the ground" (Genesis 3:19)

18 Bare, nude (Genesis 3:10)

19 "You will be like ____" (Genesis 3:5)

20 "____ reigned from Adam to Moses" (Romans 5:14)

21 ____ pain, ____ toil, ____ the sweat of your face (Genesis 3:16–17, 19)

23 Concealed, out of sight (Genesis 3:8)

26 The tempter of Eve (Genesis 3:1)

28 "You shall bruise His ____" (Genesis 3:15)

31 The tree was "____ to make one wise" (Genesis 3:6)

32 Feminine possessive pronoun (Genesis 3:6)

33 The result of judgment (Romans 5:18)

34 God placed #42 Down "____ the east of the garden" (Genesis 3:24)

36 Wickedness (Genesis 3:5)

40 The serpent was cursed to crawl on its ____ (Genesis 3:14)

41 Apparel (Genesis 3:7)

42 Angels (Genesis 3:24)

44 Earth, land (Genesis 3:17)

46 "Your ____ shall be for your husband" (Genesis 3:16)

48 Compass point (Genesis 3:24)

49 From ____ to ____ (Genesis 3:19)

51 "By the one man's offense many ____" (Romans 5:15)

53 In toil and sweat you shall ____ (Genesis 3:17–19)

*A*s our hearts go, so go our lives.

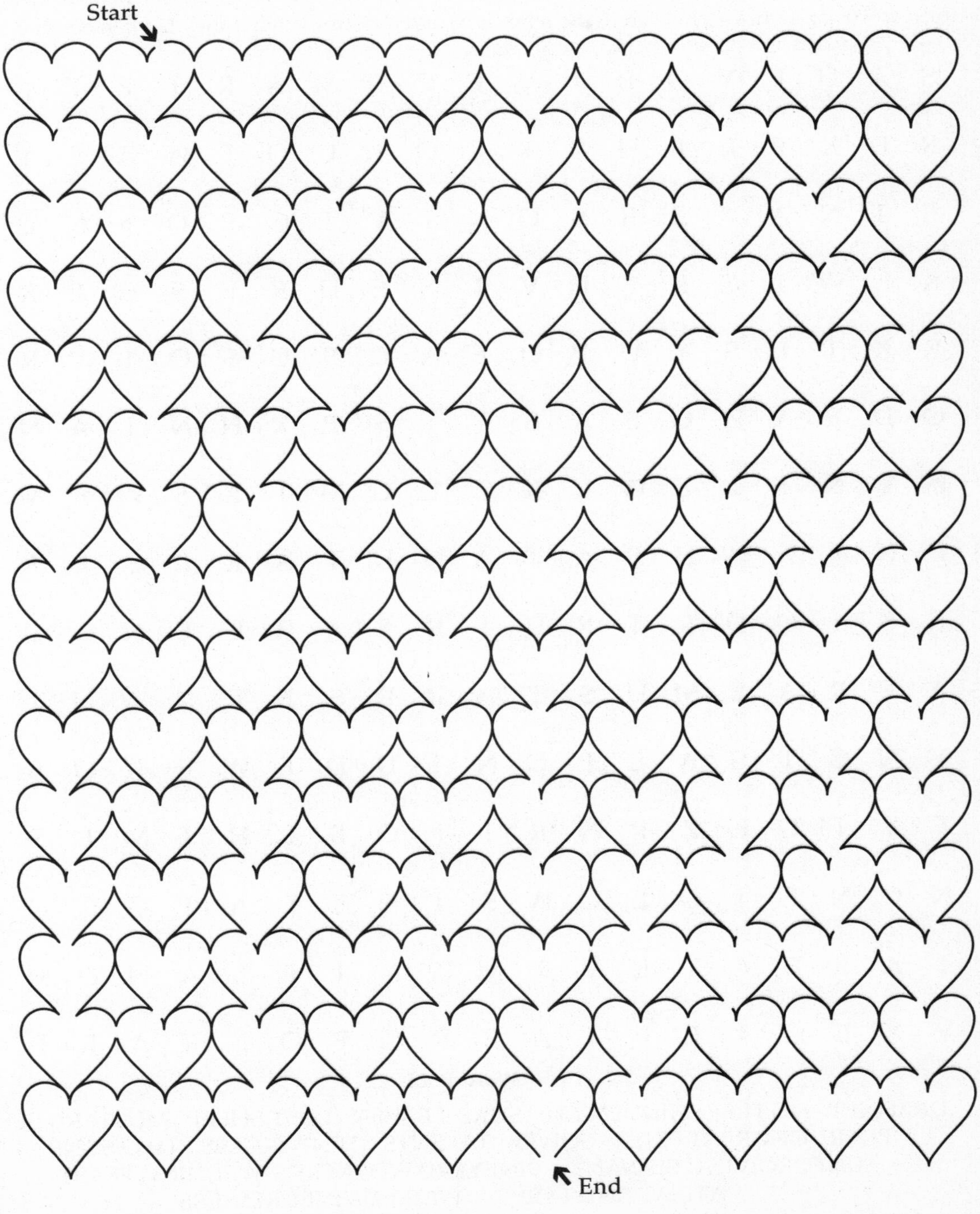

Start

End

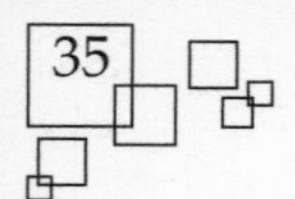

*J*esus had a way with words. He could comfort, bless, admonish, forgive, and even raise the dead with His words. There was also another way that He used words to His listeners' benefit. Find all sixteen words and phrases hidden in the letter box, and determine what they have in common.

S A U L Y O L I V E C S M A R T E F L E
R D K P E E H S T S O L U O F W A S Y R
E T N A V R E S G N I V I G R O F N U U
K U W I C K E D V I N E D R E S S E R S
R K T L S Y U P O F A C S C S O T V K A
O D E A H O B A S T I S P X H N I A N E
W E N T I E W U K Z L G M I R S W E V R
D N V X W H E A T A N D T A R E S L F T
R S I Q D R T R H J R E A R U E N A D N
A E R A E M U S T A R D S E E D W N J E
Y N G T S A E F G N I D D E W E K O B D
E V I G K Z R N R I F O B L H I M E S D
N O N E J O E O W S T N E L A T C G Q I
I A S H A T R V T M W Y I E L A N O M H
V Y E C I R P T A E R G F O L R A E P R

Word Pool

DRAGNET FIG TREE HIDDEN TREASURE LEAVEN LOST SHEEP MUSTARD SEED
PEARL OF GREAT PRICE SOWER TALENTS TEN VIRGINS TWO SONS
UNFORGIVING SERVANT VINEYARD WORKERS WEDDING FEAST
WHEAT AND TARES WICKED VINEDRESSERS

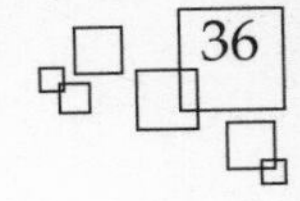

The Soils and the Seed

"Behold, a sower went out to sow," begins the parable of the sower that Jesus told to His disciples (Matthew 13:3). Jesus went on to describe four types of soil in which the seed was planted. First, there was the seed that fell by the wayside and was eaten by the birds before it had a chance to take root. Then there was the stony soil where the seed grew shallow roots but soon withered in the scorching sun. The scattered seed also took root among the thorns, but the plants were choked out when the weeds grew up around them. But the seed planted in good soil yielded thirty, sixty, and a hundredfold.

The message of the parable of the sower is timeless. When a person hears the Word of God without understanding it, the wicked one will snatch it out of the hearer's heart. For the person who receives the Word with great joy but has no depth in his heart, that one does not survive tribulation or persecution. The Word sown in a heart preoccupied with the worries and cares of the world is choked out and bears no fruit. But the Word planted in a believing, receptive heart bears fruit many times over.

Start

End

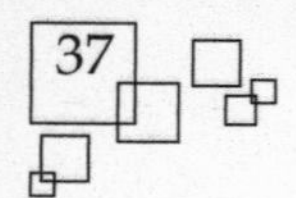

*W*hen God said "Go," Jonah said "No." But God had compassion on Jonah and the citizens of Nineveh. He spared Jonah's life, and when they repented, the Ninevites were spared the disaster that was coming to them. Find the answers to this crossword in the book of Jonah.

Across

1 Turbulence (Jonah 1:4)

4 God's command to Jonah (Jonah 1:2)

7 Jonah's nationality (Jonah 1:9)

9 Either, ____

10 Injury (Jonah 4:2)

11 Mad (Jonah 4:4)

14 Sea creature (Jonah 1:17)

15 Abyss (Jonah 2:3)

17 Still (Jonah 1:11)

18 The king of Nineveh proclaimed a fast, "Do not let them ____" (Jonah 3:7)

20 Length of Jonah's stay in the fish: ____ days and ____ nights (Jonah 1:17)
22 Jonah's mode of escape (Jonah 1:3)
23 Cinders (Jonah 3:6)
25 Center (Jonah 2:3)
27 Jonah was found fast ____ in the bottom of the ship (Jonah 1:5)
29 Chemical symbol for iron
30 Stomach (Jonah 1:17)
32 "The ____ of the Lord" (Jonah 1:1)
33 Gulp down (Jonah 1:17)
37 Sea ____ (Jonah 2:5)
39 Rescue
42 "The ____ of Nineveh believed God" (Jonah 3:5)
44 Freight (Jonah 1:5)
46 "____ have you done this?" (Jonah 1:10)
47 Number of days Nineveh residents had to repent (Jonah 3:4)
48 The Ninevites repented of this (Jonah 3:8)
50 "The ____ fell of Jonah" (Jonah 1:7)
51 More than adequate (Jonah 4:2)
53 That "great city" (Jonah 1:2)
55 First the cargo, then Jonah (Jonah 1:5, 15)
57 Ground (Jonah 1:13)
59 God's instructions to Jonah: "____ to Nineveh" (Jonah 1:2)
60 "____ is of the LORD" (Jonah 2:9)
61 "Roots" (Jonah 2:6)

Down

1 Jonah's intended destination (Jonah 1:3)
2 Die (Jonah 1:6)
3 "____ the LORD spoke to the fish" (Jonah 2:10)
5 "When my soul fainted within me, I ____ the LORD" (Jonah 2:7)
6 Shadow (Jonah 4:6)
7 Strenuously (Jonah 1:13)
8 You and I (Jonah 1:14)
9 "The belly ____ the fish" (Jonah 1:17)
12 "____, let every one turn from his evil way" (Jonah 3:8)
13 "You have brought ____ my life from the pit" (Jonah 2:6)
16 Seaport city (Jonah 1:3)
17 Stopped (Jonah 1:15)
19 "He went down ____ Joppa, and found a ship going ____ Tarshish" (Jonah 1:3)
20 Beverage made from leaves
21 Spoil
22 Place of the dead (Jonah 2:2)
24 Opposite of nights (Jonah 3:4)
26 Navigate or propel a boat with oars (past tense) (Jonah 1:13)
28 Weight, burden (Jonah 1:5)
29 "But Jonah arose to flee . . . ____ the presence of the LORD" (Jonah 1:3)
31 Jonah lamented: "It is better for me to ____ than to live" (Jonah 4:3)
34 Population of Nineveh: ____ hundred and twenty thousand persons and also much livestock (Jonah 4:11)
35 Jonah ____ faint when the sun beat on his head (Jonah 4:8)
36 God's attitude toward Nineveh (Jonah 4:11)
37 Evil (Jonah 1:2)
38 Regurgitate (Jonah 2:10)
40 Not wet (Jonah 2:10)
41 Sailing vessel
42 Proclaim (Jonah 3:2)
43 "As ____ dawned" (Jonah 4:7)
45 "God ____ ed from the disaster that He had said He would bring upon them, and He did not do it" (Jonah 3:10)
49 "Those who regard worthless ____ forsake their own Mercy" (Jonah 2:8)
51 Filled with fear (Jonah 1:10)
52 Deeds (Jonah 3:10)
54 Jonah sat on the ____ side of the city (Jonah 4:5)
55 ____ away (Jonah 3:9)
56 Creature that ate the plant that had sheltered Jonah from the sun (Jonah 4:7)
58 Lain ____ (Jonah 1:5)

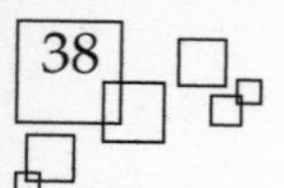

To find the names of plants and trees in the Bible, replace letters in the first word with letters from the same position in the second word. Then write the letters in the blank spaces. An example is given for you.

(F) (L) E A
H O (A) (X)

F L A X

1. C A N A A N
S U M M I T
_ _ _ _ _ _

2. R E S T
H O P E
_ _ _ _

3. L A Z Y
W I L L
_ _ _ _

4. G R U B S
H O A R D
_ _ _ _ _

5. M A N E
T I L T
_ _ _ _

6. F O X
B I G
_ _ _

7. N O I S E
A N G E L
_ _ _ _ _

8. G N O M E
W R A P S
_ _ _ _ _

9. O L D E N
D R I V E
_ _ _ _ _

10. P O E M
T A L L
_ _ _ _

11. B R I D E
G L O O M
_ _ _ _ _

12. A P S E
B L O W
_ _ _ _

13. C L E A R
M E D I A
_ _ _ _ _

14. M A P L E
A P H I D
_ _ _ _ _

15. O A R
I L K
_ _ _

16. H E A R T
M A N N A
_ _ _ _ _

17. B O A R
K E E N
_ _ _ _

18. S H O A L
W R E S T
_ _ _ _ _

19. M E L L O W
W I C K E D
_ _ _ _ _ _

20. A L L I E D
D E M O N S
_ _ _ _ _ _

21. A O R T I C
G A L L O N
_ _ _ _ _ _

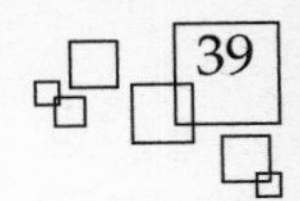

*Y*ou might think of these words of Jesus as referring to our Valentine for our Lord . . . and His gift back to us.

Clue: MESSIAH *is* ZRVVJKL

Q I R V V R M K G R

W L R E F G R J B

L R K G W' O D G W L R S

V L K I I V R R N D M.

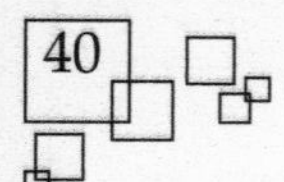

*T*he Bible frequently gives us very precise "time markers" for days, weeks, and months. Using the numbers indicated by the clues, work the equation to come up with the answer.

Clue		
Number of years children of Israel spent wandering in the desert (Numbers 32:13)	=	______
Minus . . . Number of months scorpion-like locusts are allowed to sting in the book of Revelation (Revelation 9:10)	−	______
Plus . . . Number of days two witnesses prophesy in Revelation before they are murdered (Revelation 11:3)	+	______
Divided by . . . Number of days before the murdered prophets arose (Revelation 11:11)	÷	______
Minus . . . Number of years Jeremiah prophesied Israel would serve the king of Babylon (Jeremiah 25:11)	−	______
Divided by . . . Number of days it took for God to complete His creation (Genesis 1:1–31)	÷	______
Plus . . . The day of the month that Noah's ark came to rest on Mount Ararat (Genesis 8:4)	+	______
Minus . . . Half the number of the jubilee year (Leviticus 25:10)	−	______
Minus . . . Number of months the dragon is allowed to blaspheme in Revelation (Revelation 13:5)	−	______
	=	______

*H*AND OF *R*AIN

*A*t a time of great famine in Samaria, God sent Elijah to challenge the prophets of Baal to prove before all of Israel that Elijah's God was the one true God. When the altars of Baal failed to burn and Elijah's altars were consumed, King Ahab and all of Israel rallied against the false prophets and they were executed.

Elijah had predicted God would end the devastating drought. So he sent a servant to look toward the sea for rain. When six trips produced no news of rain, Elijah sent the servant a seventh time. This time the servant reported he had seen a cloud the size of a man's hand. Elijah sent word to Ahab to ride his chariot to Jezreel to report the rain, but the spirit of God came upon Elijah and he ran on foot and beat Ahab to the city gate.

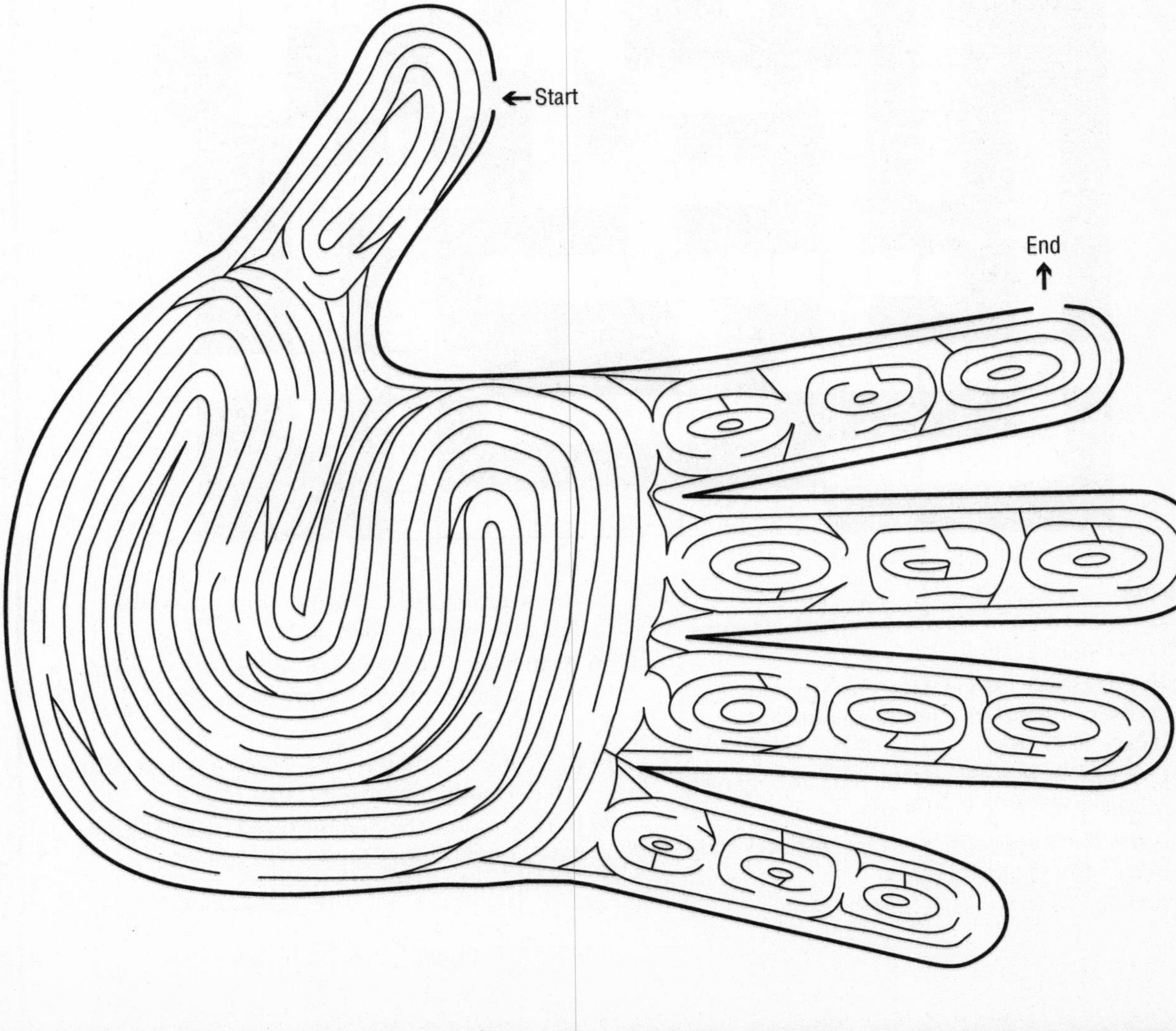

← Start

End
↑

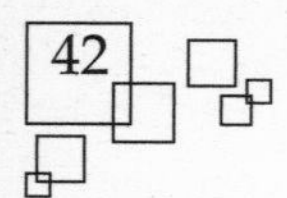

*W*hen it comes to learning more about God and receiving the blessings He has for us, it's best to sit at the feet of the Master.

Across

2 Jesus did a lot of teaching in this house of God (Mark 12:35)

6 In this city, Jesus gave the chief priests, scribes, and elders a lesson in authority (Mark 11:27–33)

8 One of two regions in which Jesus began His ministry (Matthew 4:13–16)

11 A mother's only son was brought back to life in this city (Luke 7:11–15)

12 Not yes

14 Jesus ministered to Mary in this place, after His resurrection (John 20:11)

16 At this tax collector's home, Jesus taught that it's the sick who need a physician (Luke 5:29)

17 Like

19 In a certain "small town," Martha was taught what's really important (Luke 10:38)

20 In this region, the demon-possessed daughter of a woman from Canaan was healed (Matthew 15:21–28)

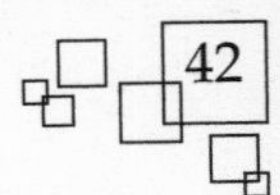

22 "But the Son of Man ____ nowhere to lay His head" (Luke 9:58)

28 Jesus healed great multitudes in this region beyond the Jordan (Matthew 19:1–2)

29 The wedding miracle took place in ____ of Galilee (John 2:1)

30 Jesus taught the devil a thing or two in this arid area (Matthew 4:1–11)

32 At Simon the leper's home in this town, Jesus taught that the poor will be with us always (Matthew 26:6–13)

33 Blind Bartimaeus was healed where Joshua once fought (Mark 10:46–52)

34 On the road to this village, Jesus opened the Scriptures to two men (Luke 24:13–35)

35 Jesus taught a lesson about healing on the Sabbath at a Pharisee ruler's "abode" (Luke 14:1–6)

36 After the demons left him for some swine, a man spread the word about Jesus in this district (Mark 5:20)

Down

1 The woman at the well learned about living water in this Samaritan city (John 4:5–10)

3 The Beatitudes were given to the disciples on one of these (Matthew 5:1–12)

4 In this type of field, the Pharisees were taught that Jesus is Lord of the Sabbath (Matthew 12:1–8)

5 The lesson in this garden was "watch and pray" (Matthew 26:36–41)

7 The sick begged to simply touch the hem of Jesus' garment in this land (Matthew 14:34–36)

9 This disciple's mother-in-law was healed in his home (Matthew 8:14–15)

10 In this country, Jesus preached that the kingdom of God was at hand (Mark 1:14–15)

13 Jesus taught His disciples the signs of the end of the age on this mountain (Matthew 24:3)

15 Jesus sat in one and taught the multitude that stood on the shore (Matthew 13:2)

18 After preaching and teaching in Galilee, Jesus healed many who lived in this province (Matthew 4:23–24)

21 The other region mentioned in conjunction with #8 Across; the two contain the town of Capernaum where Jesus dwelt (Matthew 4:13)

23 The other region connected to #20 Across; it's an ancient city of the Canaanites (Matthew 15:21)

24 In this town, Jesus claimed to be the fulfillment of Messianic prophecy (Luke 4:16–21)

25 In this people's country, Jesus healed the man whose unclean spirit was named "Legion" (Mark 5:1–9)

26 Passing through the midst of ____ and Galilee, Jesus met ten lepers and healed them; the one who thanked Him was from this city (Luke 17:12–19)

27 The Scriptures came to life when Jesus taught in this Jewish house of worship (Matthew 4:23)

31 In the Upper ____, Jesus taught His disciples the meaning of communion (Mark 14:15–25)

Bonus:
Unscramble the circled letters to find out where God meets us today.

___ ___ ___ ___ ___ ___ ___ ___ ___ ___

43

*J*esus comforted His disciples about His going away.

Clue: MESSIAH *is* JBEESDU

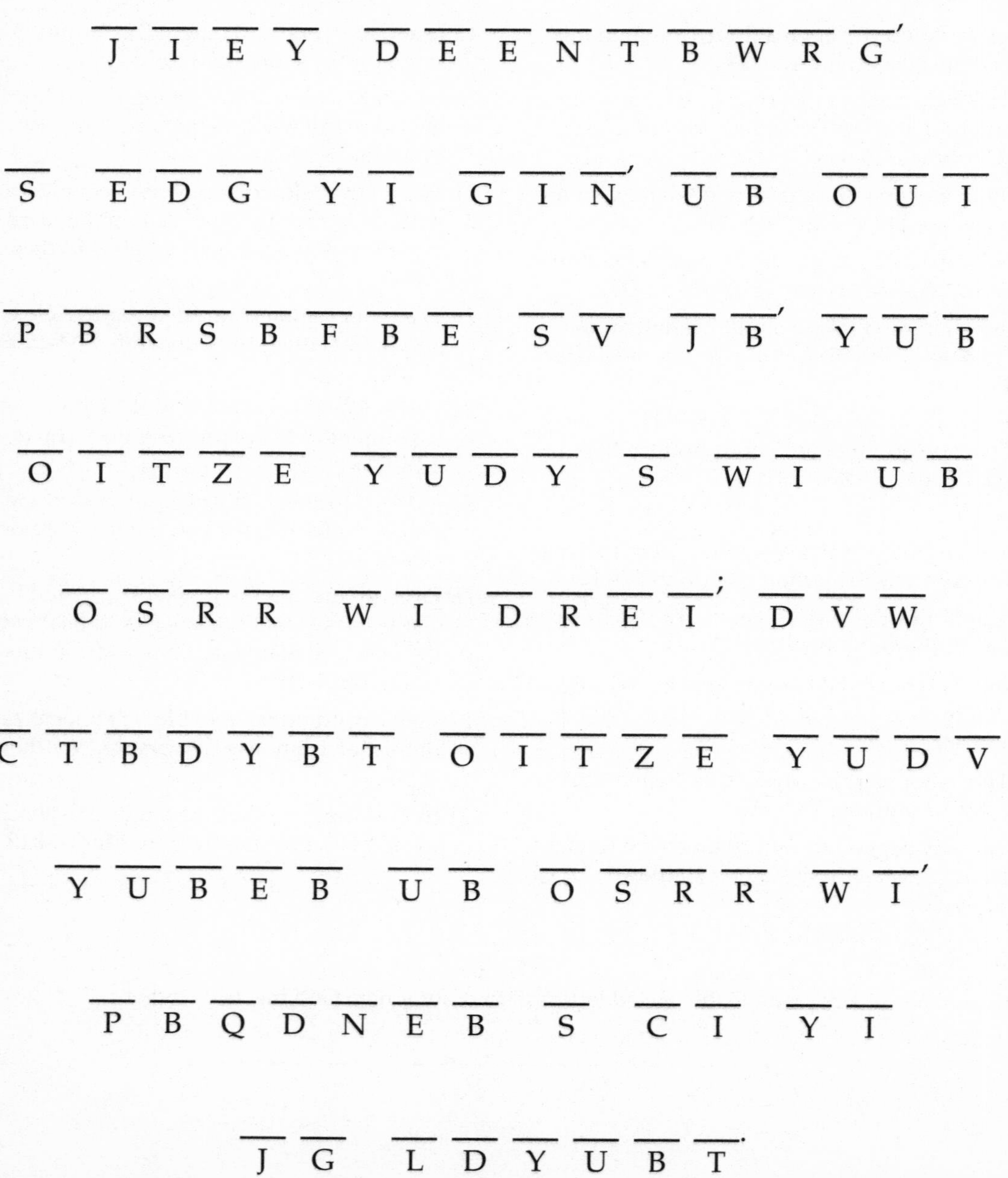

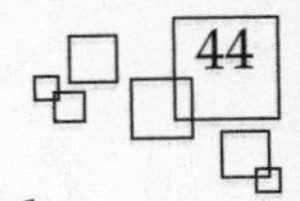

God had given us human beings the great gift of speech. That gift can be used to edify and encourage other people—or it can be misused to destroy or hurt people. The words in this puzzle concern Bible references to our misuse of speech—specifically, the ability to start small-scale and large-scale wars.

A R N S V K F X G B R E K J W D T O W P

D L O I D T C L U I E N R E P I V B I O

T Q I E K H Y G I C I S P S P C R N C A

E W T Q H I H C N V Q V S W O R D S K Z

C G A F N X Z E E S E J C O I B S Y E N

L M N G Q C L S T S R X L R S M R A D A

T F G Y S O U V R F M B P R O U A F N Z

Y K I V I O W E A R R O G A N C E K E Q

I E D V R G V O U A P S K L N H P J S M

M N N H J R O D Z J B I S E D I S V S V

P F I R E U H O D E S T R U C T I O N X

O R T P E G R U O C S L K N W M A Y M W

E K G X L E U Z J P Y D W F I B G N Z A

Word Pool

ARROGANCE ARROWS DESTRUCTION EVIL FIRE INDIGNATION KNIVES LYING PERVERSE POISON RAZOR SCOURGE SMOKE SPEARS SWORDS VIOLENCE VIPER WICKEDNESS

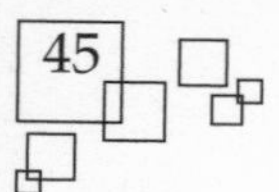

*T*he Israelites didn't know much about winning friends, but they definitely influenced people. This puzzle concerns many of the kings (and their nations) who fought the Israelites.

Across

1 The king of the land was hanged on a tree untill evening (Joshua 8:29)

3 One of the kings of Midian; the death of his daughter, Cozbi, stopped the plague in Israel (Numbers 25:6–15)

4 The king of this town was struck with the edge of the sword (Joshua 11:1, 10)

6 A town in the territory of Judah, near the place where David and Goliath fought (Joshua 12:15)

9 The king of Jarmuth (Joshua 10:3)

14 Another king of Midian; his name means "desirous" (Numbers 31:8)

15 A town near Mount Carmel; its name means "possession of the people" (Joshua 12:22)

16 The king of this country wouldn't let Moses and the Israelites pass through (Numbers 20:14–21)

18 King of Hebron (Joshua 10:3)

19 The king of this city wanted Rahab to squeal on the Israelite spies (Joshua 2:3)

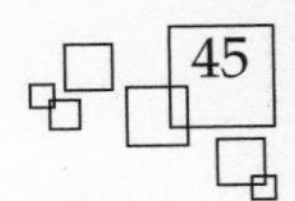

21 This city of Canaan was captured by Joshua (Joshua 11:1–8)

23 King of Hazor (Joshua 11:1)

24 For example

27 Meaning "sacred place," this town in south Judah and its king were conquered by Joshua (Joshua 12:22)

28 Another king of Midian; his name means "friendship" (Numbers 31:8)

29 The king of this city met the same fate as the king of #19 Across (Joshua 10:28)

30 This city (and its king), conquered by Joshua, was later given to the Levites (Joshua 12:13)

Down

1 The king of this city fought against Israel and took some of them prisoner; the name means "fugitive" (Numbers 21:1)

2 A Canaanite town in the territory of Asher; its name means "habitation" (Joshua 11:2; 12:23)

4 Another king of Midian (Numbers 31:8)

6 How many kings of Midian were there? (Numbers 31:8)

7 A Canaanite city near Lachish; its name means "whiteness" (Joshua 10:29–30)

8 Military police (abbr.)

10 The king of Jerusalem in Joshua's time; his name means "My Lord is righteous" (2 words) (Joshua 10:1)

11 This king of Heshbon would not grant passage to the Israelites (Deuteronomy 2:30)

12 This city, "devoted to destruction," was destroyed by Israel (Numbers 21:1–3)

13 Meaning "pit" or "well," this town west of Jordan was another Israelite conquest (Joshua 12:17)

17 This king of Bashan fought Israel at Edrel (Numbers 21:33)

19 King of Lachish; his name means "may He (God) cause to shine forth" (Joshua 10:3)

20 A town near Samaria; its name means "delight" (Joshua 12:24)

21 This king fought with Israel in Rephidim; his name means "warlike" (Exodus 17:8)

22 A town in Judah; its name means "fence" (Joshua 12:13)

23 This king of Madon has a name that means "to call loudly" (Joshua 11:1)

25 Horam, this city's king, came to the aid of Lachish, but was struck down (Joshua 10:33)

26 Another king of Midian (Numbers 31:8)

Bonus:
Unscramble the circled letters to form four words that tell of the ultimate victor all Christians are eagerly awaiting.

__ __ __   __ __ __ __   __ __   __ __ __ __ __ __

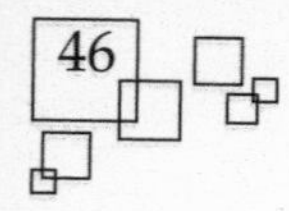

Safe Passage

Genesis 6:14—9:17 gives us a remarkable account of a man's faith in God in the face of seemingly ridiculous instructions. Not only did God tell Noah that it was going to rain (a phenomenon heretofore unknown), but that he was to save himself, his family, and a pair of every animal species by building a huge boat.

God was very specific about how the ark was to be built giving specific materials (gopherwood and pitch), size (450 feet long, seventy-five feet wide, and forty-five feet high), and arrangement (three decks, a door in the side with a window). Scholars have calculated that a vessel of this size would hold about forty-three thousand tons.

The rain lasted forty days and nights covering the earth with water for 150 days. Several accounts from the ancient world (other than the Scriptures) record stories of the Flood and some even recount versions of Noah's ark.

After almost a year on the water, the ark came to rest on Mount Ararat in what is now Turkey. Various attempts to locate the ark's remains have not uncovered indisputable evidence that the ark still exists. However, several archaeologists, who have braved shifting glaciers and dangerously unpredictable weather in their explorations, still claim that the ark may be caught beneath the ice.

Start

End

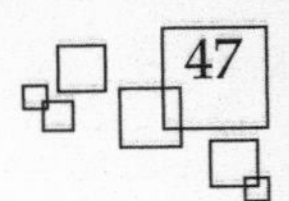

*I*n this puzzle, you'll explore the ages of our long-lived biblical ancestors.

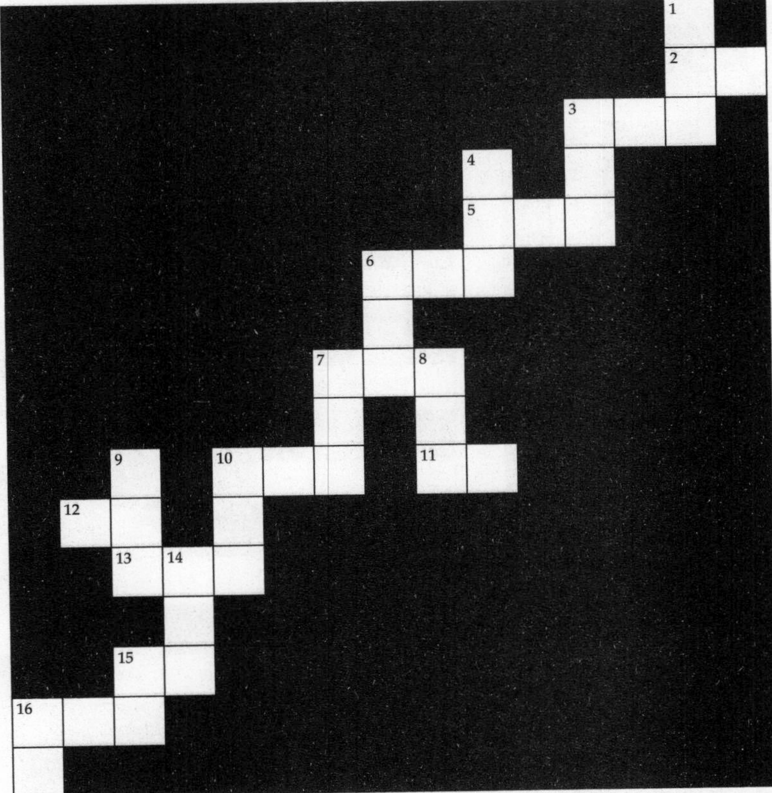

Across

2 The age of Isaac when Esau and Jacob were born (Genesis 25:25–26)

3 The age of Enosh at his death (Genesis 5:11)

5 The age of Cainan at his death (Genesis 5:14)

6 The age of Abraham at his death (Genesis 25:7)

7 The age of Sarah at her death (Genesis 23:1)

10 The age of Adam at his death (Genesis 5:5)

11 The age of Abram when he departed from Haran for the land God had promised him (Genesis 12:4)

12 The age of Abram when Hagar gave birth to Ishmael (Genesis 16:16)

13 The age of Jared at his death (Genesis 5:20)

15 The age of Isaac when he took Rebekah as a wife (Genesis 25:20)

16 The age of Joseph at his death (Genesis 50:26)

Down

1 The age of Enoch when he "walked with God" (Genesis 5:23)

3 The age of Noah at his death (Genesis 9:29)

4 The age of Mahalalel at his death (Genesis 5:17)

6 The age of Lamech when Noah was born (Genesis 5:28)

7 The age of Adam when Seth was born (Genesis 5:3)

8 The age of Lamech at his death (Genesis 5:31)

9 The age of Methuselah at his death (Genesis 5:27)

10 The age of Seth at his death (Genesis 5:8)

14 The age of Noah when the floodwaters came on the earth (Genesis 7:6)

15 The age of Esau when he took Judith and Basemath as wives (Genesis 26:34)

16 The age of Joseph when God gave him dreams of his destiny (Genesis 37:2)

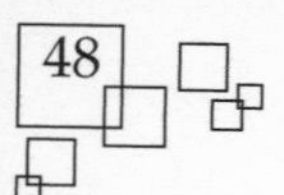

*T*hink "BiblES," and this one will be easier!

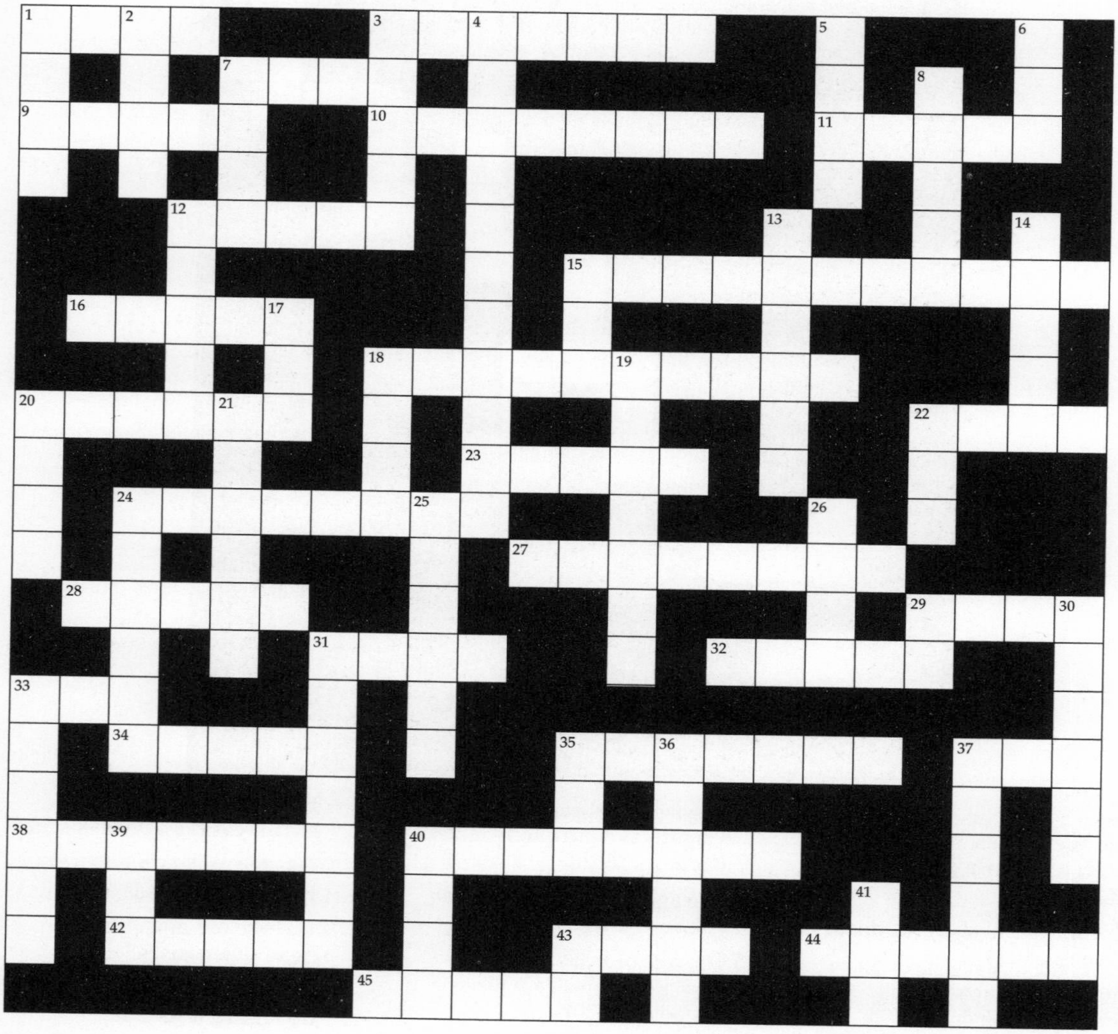

Across

1 Shem was the father "of all the children of ____" (Genesis 10:21)

3 Fourth foundation jewel of New Jerusalem (Revelation 21:19)

7 Paul said Jesus became obedient to "____ the death of the cross" (Philippians 2:8)

9 The Jews sought to kill Jesus because they perceived He made Himself "____ with God" (John 5:18)

10 Jacob hid them under the terebinth tree by Shechem (Genesis 35:4)

11 Age, in days, of a male child when he is to be circumcised (Genesis 17:12)

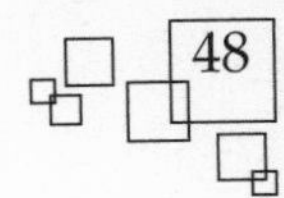

12 In Mary's song, the Lord sends the rich away in this state (Luke 1:53)

15 Unending

16 To expand is to en____

18 One of the five ministry callings set in the church (Ephesians 4:11)

20 King Ahasuerus' queen (Esther 2:7)

22 Priest and scribe; fifteenth book of the Old Testament

23 David made him an officer over the tribe of Judah (1 Chronicles 27:18)

24 New Testament letters

27 Paul called him a "fellow prisoner in Christ Jesus" (Philemon 23)

28 About a bushel, in Hebrew measurement

29 The one of a sword is to be avoided!

31 ____ and every one

32 "____ into His gates with thanksgiving" (Psalm 100:4)

33 The writer of Proverbs said, "Lend your ____ to my understanding" (Proverbs 5:1)

34 One of King David's wives (2 Samuel 3:5)

35 One of Aaron's sons, he ministered as a priest (Numbers 3:4)

37 High priest whom Samuel served (1 Samuel 1:25)

38 David and Goliath, for example

40 Phillip explained the Scriptures to a eunuch from this nation (Acts 8:27)

42 Another name for Elijah

43 Red; another name for Esau (Genesis 25:30)

44 "They shall fear You as long as the sun and moon ____" (Psalm 72:5)

45 Peter wrote, "You younger people, submit yourselves to your ____" (sing.) (1 Peter 5:5)

Down

1 First garden

2 The name of the month (Hebrew) in which Nehemiah's wall was finished (Nehemiah 6:15)

3 Adversary

4 Jesus prophesied they will be part of "the beginning of sorrows" (Matthew 24:7–8)

5 The psalmist said he lifted his to the hills "from whence comes my help" (Psalm 121:1)

6 A woman of Canaan said to Jesus, "Even the little dogs ____ the crumbs which fall from their masters' table" (Matthew 15:27)

7 Place with twelve wells and seventy palm trees (Exodus 15:27)

8 Land of bondage (Exodus 3:16–17)

12 The psalmist declared it is full of the Lord's possessions (Psalm 104:24)

13 Receiver of a double portion of Elijah's spirit (2 Kings 2:9)

14 King Saul asked a woman from here to conjure the spirit of Samuel (2 words) (1 Samuel 28:7)

15 Job said the white of one is tasteless (Job 6:6)

17 To make a mistake

18 The Lord taught us to pray for deliverance from "the ____ one" (Matthew 6:13)

19 It is called "the helmet for My head" (Psalm 60:7)

20 Direction from which the wise men came (Matthew 2:1)

21 His trip to heaven was via a fiery chariot and whirlwind (2 Kings 2:11)

22 "From the ____ of the earth I will cry to You" (Psalm 61:2)

24 Ahasuerus made a decree "throughout all his ____" that wives are to honor their husbands (Esther 1:20)

25 Valley of great grapes (Numbers 13:23–24)

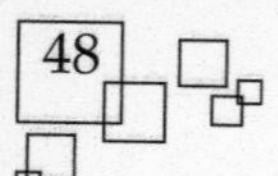

26 The Lord "placed cherubim at the ____ of the garden of Eden" (Genesis 3:24)

29 Judah's eldest son (Genesis 38:6)

30 Timothy's mother (2 Timothy 1:5)

31 City of Ephesians

33 David's hiding place (2 words) (1 Samuel 23:29)

35 His sons Hophni and Phinehas were killed when the ark of God was captured (1 Samuel 4:16–17)

36 Hire

37 After His resurrection, Jesus walked with two men on the road to this village (Luke 24:13)

39 Adam's helpmate (Genesis 3:20)

40 Mountain on which Joshua built an altar (Joshua 8:30)

41 Alpha and Omega, Beginning and ____ (Revelation 21:6)

43 Firstborn son of Judah and Shua (Genesis 38:3)

*H*elp is on the way.

Clue: **MESSIAH *is* NGHHRST**

QZF UG WZ XZM TSAG

S TRVT CFRGHM UTZ

KSXXZM HLNCSMTRBG

URMT ZEF UGSIXGHHGH,

DEM USH RX SPP CZRXMH

MGNCMGW SH UG SFG, LGM

URMTZEM HRX. PGM EH

MTGFGQZFG KZNG

DZPWPL MZ MTG MTFZXG

ZQ VFSKG, MTSM UG NSL

ZDMSRX NGFKL SXW QRXW

VFSKG MZ TGPC RX MRNG

ZQ XGGW.

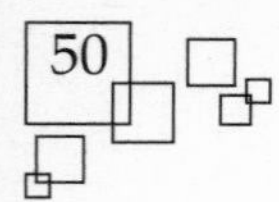

*T*HE *P*ATRIARCHAL *C*ROSS

*T*his cross shape is an elaboration of the basic Latin cross, which has been adapted in more than four hundred ways as a Christian symbol.

The short arm at the top of the cross represents the placard on which Pilate wrote, "Jesus of Nazareth, the King of the Jews" (John 19:19). When used today, the short arm often bears the inscription "I. N. R. I." which stands for the Latin translation of his placard: "Iesus Nazarenus Rex ludaeorum."

In early paintings, church patriarchs are frequently shown carrying this cross as a means of identifying with the cross of Jesus. The cross later became a symbol used by the cardinals and archbishops of the church. This cross shape is also associated with Peter and Philip.

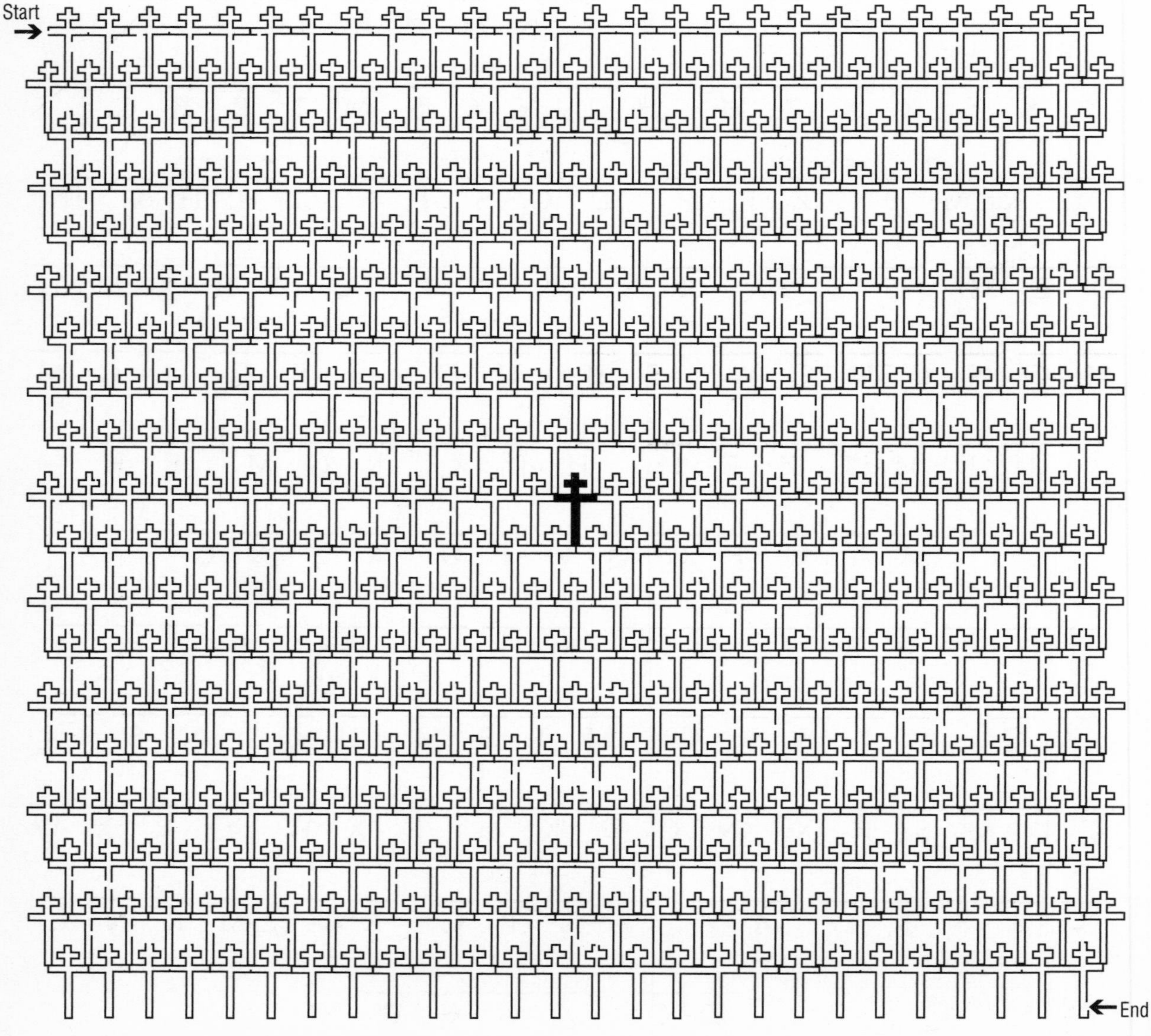

Start →

← End

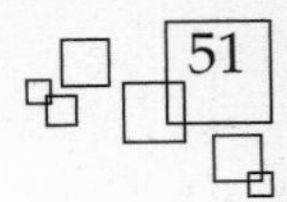

*E*xploring the possibilities . . .

Connect the letters—in all directions—to form a word string that gives one of the most famous quotes of Jesus.

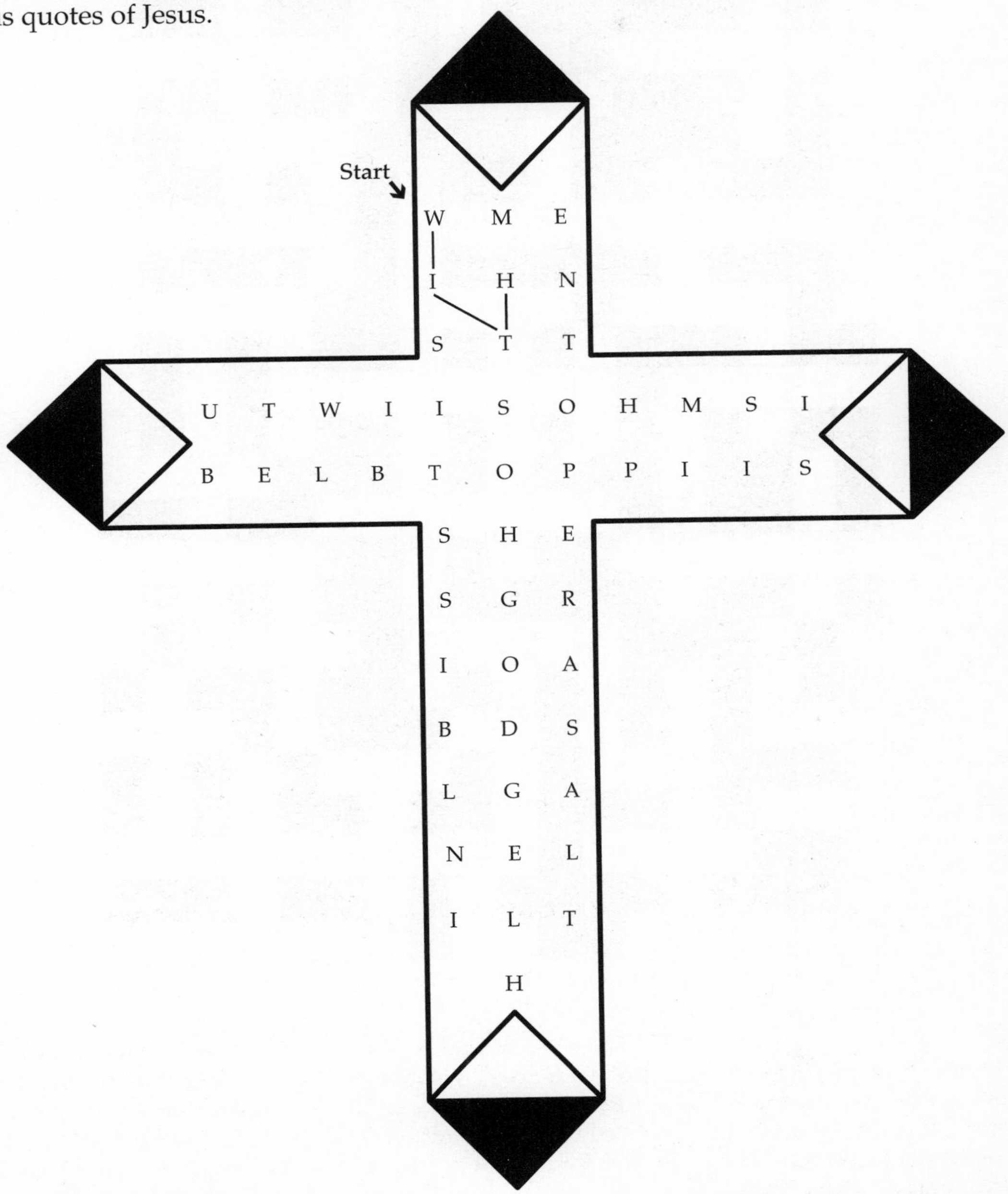

Start

W M E

I H N

S T T

U T W I I S O H M S I

B E L B T O P P I I S

S H E

S G R

I O A

B D S

L G A

N E L

I L T

H

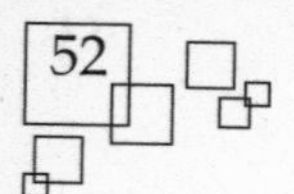

*T*he words to complete this crossword are all about the Word of God.

Across

1 "The words of the LORD are pure . . . like ____ tried in a furnace of earth" (Psalm 12:6)

3 "The word of God is #7 Across and ____" (Hebrews 4:12)

7 "The word of God is ____ and #3 Across" (Hebrews 4:12)

9 "You have the words of ____ life" (John 6:68)

10 "These are written that you may believe . . . and that believing you may have ____" (John 20:31)

11 "Receive . . . the implanted word, which is able to ____ your souls" (James 1:21)

15 "All Scripture is given by ____ of God" (2 Timothy 3:16)
16 "I will not ____ Your word" (Psalm 119:16)
17 "The ____ is the word of God" (Luke 8:11)
18 "The Holy Scriptures, which are ____ to make you wise for salvation" (2 Timothy 3:15)
20 "The word is near you, in your mouth and in your ____" (Romans 10:8)
23 "Your word is ____" (John 17:17)
25 "I rejoice at Your word as one who finds great ____" (Psalm 119:162)
27 "Be diligent to present yourself approved to God, a worker who ____ not need to be ashamed, rightly dividing the word of truth" (2 Timothy 2:15)
28 "How can a young man ____ his way? By taking heed according to Your word" (Psalm 119:9)
29 "Your word I have ____ in my heart, that I might not sin against You" (Psalm 119:11)
30 "The word of His grace, which is able to ____ you up" (Acts 20:32)
34 "Born ____ . . . through the word of God" (1 Peter 1:23)
36 "The word is ____ near you" (Deuteronomy 30:14)
39 "All Scripture is given . . . that the ____ of God may be complete, thoroughly equipped for every good work" (2 Timothy 3:16–17)
40 " ____ that day the deaf shall hear the words of the book" (Isaiah 29:18)
41 "He wrote on the tablets the words of the covenant, the ____ Commandments" (Exodus 34:28)
42 "Your word was to me the ____ and rejoicing of my heart" (Jeremiah 15:16)
43 "If you #35 Down in Me, and My words #35 Down in you, you will ____ what you desire, and it shall be done for you" (John 15:7)
46 "I will ____ forget Your word" (Psalm 119:16)
47 "The testimony of the LORD is sure, making ____ the simple" (Psalm 19:7)
48 "____ me according to Your word" (Psalm 119:28)
50 "Is not My word . . . like a ____ that breaks the rock in pieces?" (Jeremiah 23:29)
51 "If anyone loves Me, he will keep My word; and My Father will love him, and We will come ____ him and make Our home with him" (John 14:23)
52 "The word of God is . . . ____ than any two-edged sword" (Hebrews 4:12)

Down

1 "Your ____ according to Your word" (Psalm 119:41)
2 "If anyone ____ Me, he will keep My word" (John 14:23)
3 "Every word of God is ____" (Proverbs 30:5)
4 "'Do not mourn nor ____.' For all the people wept, when they heard the words of the Law" (Nehemiah 8:9)
5 "But the word of the LORD endures ____" (1 Peter 1:25)
6 "Speak . . . ____ the words that I command you to speak to them" (Jeremiah 26:2)
8 "Your word is . . . a ____ to my path" (Psalm 119:105)
11 "Hold me up, and I shall be ____, and I shall observe Your statutes continually" (Psalm 119:117)
12 "Is not My word like a ____?" (Jeremiah 23:29)
13 "The entrance of Your words gives light; it gives ____ to the simple" (Psalm 119:130)
14 "The ____ of the LORD are right" (Psalm 19:8)
17 "Piercing even to the division of ____ and spirit" (Hebrews 4:12)
19 "____ are those who keep His testimonies" (Psalm 119:2)
20 "Whoever . . . does not ____ your words . . . shall be put to death" (Joshua 1:18)
21 "His word was with ____" (Luke 4:32)
22 "Your words were found, and I ____ them" (Jeremiah 15:16)
24 "Forever, O LORD, Your word is settled in ____" (Psalm 119:89)
26 "My word . . . shall not return to Me ____" (Isaiah 55:11)
30 "Man shall not live by ____ alone; but . . . by every word that proceeds from the mouth of the LORD" (Deuteronomy 8:3)
31 "To____ this Scripture is fulfilled in your hearing" (Luke 4:21)
32 "Do not ____ a word" (Jeremiah 26:2)
33 "Rivers of water run down from my eyes, because ____ do not keep Your law" (Psalm 119:136)
34 "My words will by no means pass ____" (Matthew 24:35)
35 "If you ____ in Me, and My words ____ in you" (John 15:7)
37 "I ____ at Your word" (Psalm 119:162)
38 "Great ____ have those who love Your law" (Psalm 119:165)
44 "Direct my ____ by Your word" (Psalm 119:133)
45 "Christ also loved the church and gave Himself for her, that He might sanctify and cleanse her with the washing of ____ by the word" (Ephesians 5:25–26)
49 "Cut ____ tablets of stone . . . and I will write on these tablets the words" (Exodus 34:1)

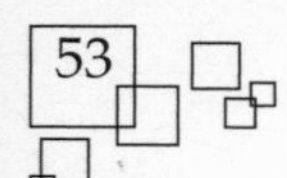

*T*he letter grid below contains twelve words associated with salt in the Bible. See how many you can find before consulting the Scripture Pool.

C E Y T R A E S P V T S Y

S H R E C F I G I A F T O

S A T X I Y C N F L I B G

H W C R A L L I P L L P F

C L E R A P D R T E S A L

E O B N I E L E N Y I L V

E P D O E C I F I R C A S

P R I F L A V F N A L V C

S T I P L N B O W L E E H

Scripture Pool

GENESIS 14:3 GENESIS 19:26 LEVITICUS 2:13 DEUTERONOMY 29:23
JOSHUA 15:62 2 SAMUEL 8:13 2 KINGS 2:20 ZEPHANIAH 2:9 MATTHEW 5:13
MARK 9:49 COLOSSIANS 4:6

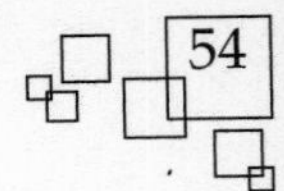

A diplomat's heritage?

Clue: MESSIAH *is* PSWWJGR

Y F S W W S H   G N S   U R S

V S G T S P G Q S N W'   I E N

U R S L   W R G F F   Y S

T G F F S H   W E O W

E I   Z E H.

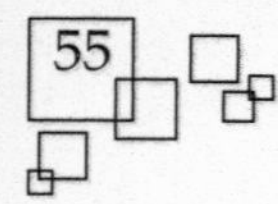

Tax Collecting

Luke 19 gives us an unusual account of a man named Zacchaeus. He was the chief tax collector in the city of Jericho. Tax collectors, in general, were hated, since their "salaries" were collected along with the taxes. Most tax collectors were considered little better than extortionists. Zacchaeus, as the chief collector, was probably one of the most hated, but he was also probably one of the richest men in the city.

Knowing his own reputation, Zacchaeus only hoped to catch a glimpse of Jesus as He passed by. Because he was short, Zacchaeus ran ahead of the crowd and climbed into a sycamore tree to get a better vantage point. Imagine the shock of the crowd—and Zacchaeus, too—when Jesus stopped beneath the tree and bade Zacchaeus to come down, and informed him that He should be Zacchaeus's guest. Jesus' action caused a dramatic change in the life of Zacchaeus and his family. He distributed much of his wealth to the poor, sought to right past wrongs, and began to follow the Master.

Jesus said, "The Son of Man has come to seek and to save that which was lost" (Luke 19:10).

Beginning at Zacchaeus, travel to each house to collect taxes. You must pass through each house to the adjacent street to continue the task. You can only go to each house once and you cannot double back or cross over the path you have already taken. Then finish up at the tree.

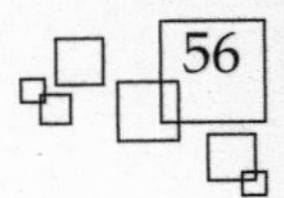

A nice place to visit? Not these cities and towns. Not if you worshiped the one true God and didn't go in for idolatry, fornication, and other commandment breakers.

Across

4 Another name for #17 Across (Jeremiah 46:14)

6 This city was "the beginning of sin" to the daughter of Zion (poss.) (Micah 1:13)

9 After seventy years, this city will commit fornication with all the kingdoms of the world (Isaiah 23:17)

12 In Abraham's day, the outcry against this city was great (Genesis 18:20)

13 The sword of the Lord is filled with blood; there's a great slaughter in this land (Isaiah 34:6)

15 The young men of this city and of Pi Beseth "shall fall by the sword" (Ezekiel 30:17)

16 It "will cease from being a city, and . . . will be a ruinous heap" (Isaiah 17:1)

17 This ancient capital of Egypt "shall be waste and desolate" (Jeremiah 44:1; 46:19; Hosea 9:6)

19 God will turn His hand against this Philistine city (Amos 1:8)

20 God will show the nations the nakedness of this city (Nahum 3:5–7)

22 The goddess Astarte was worshiped in this capital of Og, land of giants (Deuteronomy 1:4; Joshua 13:12)

24 Solomon foolishly worshiped Ashtoreth, the goddess of this city (1 Kings 11:5; Isaiah 23:12)

Down

1 Manasseh allowed the Canaanites to remain in this town just north of Caesarea; its king was conquered by Joshua (Judges 1:27)

2 Though "exalted to heaven," it will be "brought down to Hades" (Matthew 11:23)

3 The Philistine idol Dagon was worshiped here (1 Samuel 5:1–2)

4 New York (abbr.)

5 Eating things sacrificed to idols was one sin in this Revelation city (Revelation 2:12, 14)

7 #12 Across's partner in crime

8 "The beauty of the Chaldeans' pride" will never be inhabited after God is through with it (Isaiah 13:19–20)

10 Joy and gladness are taken from this land (Jeremiah 48:33)

11 Jesus renounced this city for its unbelief (Matthew 11:21)

14 God will make it "a heap of ruins in the field" (Micah 1:6)

15 God appointed His sword against this Philistine city and "against the seashore" (Jeremiah 47:7)

18 It didn't turn to persecuting Christians in a day (Acts 28:16)

21 Another name for Ava, a people who worshiped Nibhaz and Tartak (2 Kings 17:24, 31; 18:34)

23 Another name for Aven and Heliopolis, it means the opposite of "off." Its people were sun worshipers (Genesis 41:45, 50)

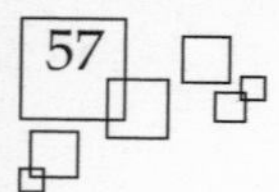

*T*he prophetess Deborah sat under her own palm tree as Israel made its way to her for judgments. (See Judges 4.)

Start

End

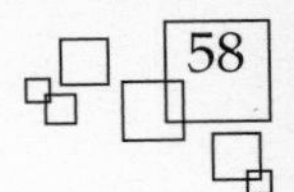

*T*he apostle Paul rarely traveled or ministered by himself. In the box of letters below, find the names of thirteen men and women who worked alongside Paul in the spreading of the gospel and the founding of the early chruch. (See Acts 12:25; 13:2, 5; 15:40; 18:18; 19:22, 29; 20:4 for help.)

A S U H C R A T S I R A S P K

R H O P O R T E I U Q O S R A

I A C P N S C J O H P A A I M

S R S U A U A U I A G M L S Y

A S E U N T H B T L L A I C H

T Q U D C P E R A S T U S I T

R M U A D I O R C N P B A L O

A S U I A G H U E H R I R L M

M B A R L R N C S O I A U A I

A A L I S A D T Y J S Q B N T

R S U M I H P O R T A S U B A

Word Pool

AQUILA ARISTARCHUS BARNABAS ERASTUS GAIUS MARK PRISCILLA SECUNDUS SILAS SOPATER TIMOTHY TROPHIMUS TYCHICUS

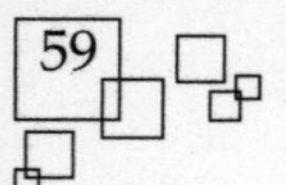

*S*ustenance is available to those who obey God.

Clue: MESSIAH is VRCCGTW

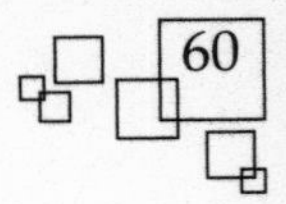

*E*VANGELIZING

*T*hese are some of the places Paul visited on his three missionary trips. On his first trip he visited Antioch, where he was rejected by the Jews. At the conclusion of that trip, he and Barnabas went to Jerusalem, where they testified before the council about all that God had done. The second trip included Philippi, where Lydia was converted, and Corinth, where he established a church. In Galatia, on the third trip, Paul worked to help build up the church.

Start

JERUSALEM
ANTIOCH
PHILIPPI
CORINTH
GALATIA

End

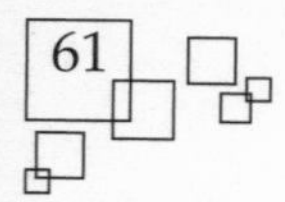

Noah, Lot, Moses, David, Daniel, Shadrach, Meshach, Abed-Nego, and even Jesus Himself are among those who were rescued by God's mighty arm of deliverance in some very perilous circumstances. Fill in the grid below with words from those stories in the Bible.

Across

1 Grieved (Genesis 6:6)

4 "The LORD ____ that the wickedness of man was great in the earth" (Genesis 6:5)

9 Daniel's prayer posture (Daniel 6:10)

12 "Stand still, and see the ____ of the LORD," (Exodus 14:13)

14 Chosen to lead God's rescue of His people from Egypt (Exodus 3:4, 10)

16 God delivered the Israelites in battle against this army (Exodus 17:13)

17 "The LORD ____ all the firstborn in the land" (Exodus 13:15, KJV)

18 "There is no other God who can ____ like this" (Daniel 3:29)

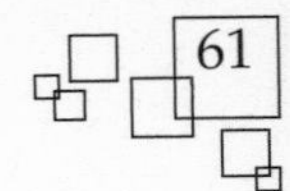

24 Also known as (abbr.)

25 An angel warned Joseph in a ____ to escape with Mary and Jesus to Egypt (Matthew 2:13)

28 "Why ____ you cry to Me?" (Exodus 14:15)

29 Compassion (Genesis 19:19)

30 "Who is like ____, O LORD?" (Exodus 15:11)

31 Moses ____ down when his hands got heavy (Exodus 17:12)

33 Abraham's nephew saved from destruction of Sodom and Gomorrah (Genesis 19:29)

35 Those who were bitten and looked at the serpent on the pole "shall ____" (Numbers 21:8)

37 God's promise to Noah (Genesis 6:18)

39 Those who disobeyed King Nebuchadnezzar were sentenced to die in the ____ (Daniel 3:15)

40 Either, ____

42 God said He would "harden the ____ of the Egyptians" (Exodus 14:17)

43 Daniel's companions in the den (Daniel 6:16)

45 Nebuchadnezzar was so angry when his decree was disobeyed that "the expression on his ____ changed" (Daniel 3:19)

47 Leave out

48 Nourishment, sustenance (Genesis 6:21)

49 Where Lot was sitting when the angels came to Sodom (Genesis 19:1)

50 "Come ____ before the LORD" (Exodus 16:9)

51 To save his life, he hid in the Wilderness of Ziph (1 Samuel 23:14)

52 "Our God whom we serve is able ____ deliver us" (Daniel 3:17)

53 During the drought the ravens provided this prophet with food and water (1 Kings 17:1, 4)

54 City where Lot and his family escaped to (Genesis 19:22)

55 Noah and Moses built these structures (sing.) to remember the Lord's deliverance (Genesis 8:20; Exodus 17:15)

58 The number of men walking in the fire (Daniel 3:25)

60 "The children of Israel complained ____ Moses and Aaron in the wilderness" (Exodus 16:2)

62 The lions' mouths were closed, ____ that they might not hurt Daniel (Daniel 6:22)

63 When Lot looked toward Sodom and Gomorrah, he saw "the ____ of the land which went up like the ____ of a furnace" (Genesis 19:28)

64 Tendency

65 "My God sent His angel and ____ the lions' mouths" (Daniel 6:22)

68 "The children of Israel went out with ____" (Exodus 14:8)

71 Dried grape

72 The people complained against Moses that they would die of ____ in the wilderness (Exodus 17:3)

74 "When Moses held ____ his hand, . . . Israel prevailed" (Exodus 17:11)

76 Fermented dough (Exodus 12:15)

77 Noah ___ according to what God commanded him (Genesis 6:22)

78 God promised Noah that He would not again ___ every living thing (Genesis 8:21)

79 "They baked unleavened ____ [sing.] . . . because they were driven out of Egypt" (Exodus 12:39)

Down

1 King Darius said, "Your God, whom you ____ continually, He will deliver you" (Daniel 6:16)

2 Male sheep

3 Affirmative

5 "____ the LORD commanded" (Exodus 16:34)

6 The ____ (sing.) covered the chariots, horsemen, and Pharaoh's army (Exodus 14:28)

7 "At ____ ye shall eat flesh" (Exodus 16:12, KJV)

8 "The earth was filled with ____" (adj.) (Genesis 6:11)

9 "That the Egyptians may ____ that I am the LORD" (Exodus 14:4)

10 The houses marked with the blood of the ____ would not suffer the death of the firstborn (Exodus 12:5–7, 13)

11 God's provision of escape for Noah and his family (Genesis 6:14)

13 King Saul "conspired" evil toward David (present tense) (1 Samuel 23:9)

15 The thoughts of man's heart was "only ____ continually" (Genesis 6:5)

19 Land of bondage and oppression for children of Israel

20 Filled with raging jealousy, this Israelite king was obsessed with killing his apparent successor (1 Samuel 23:15)

21 The Israelite would eat in ____ with their sandals, belts, and staffs (Exodus 12:11)

22 The fire had no ____, because God delivered the Hebrew children (Daniel 3:27)

23 Pharaoh's words to the Israelites: "____ ____" (2 words) (Exodus 12:32)

26 "____ for your life!" (Genesis 19:17)

27 The sacrificial lamb was to be "a ____ of the first year" (Exodus 12:5)

32 Jewish festival commemorating God's deliverance of His people from slavery (Exodus 12:11, 14)

34 God's miraculous provision to the children of Israel and Elijah (Exodus 16:4; 1 Kings 17:6)

36 "Heed the ____ of the LORD" (Exodus 15:26)

38 Daniel's enemies could find no ____ in him (Daniel 6:4)

39 God caused the ____ in judgment against the evil and violence on the earth (Genesis 6:17)

41 "They [the serpents] ____ the people" (Numbers 21:6)

42 God's instrument of deliverance (Exodus 13:9)

43 Two of every ____ thing were brought in the ark (Genesis 6:19)

44 He "found grace in the eyes of the LORD" (Genesis 6:8)

45 The Lord granted the people ____ in the sight of the Egyptians (Exodus 12:36)

46 "____ the end of the hundred and fifty days the waters decreased" (Genesis 8:3)

48 "The LORD will ____ for you" (Exodus 14:14)

51 This Hebrew prince was miraculously delivered, but his enemies perished (Daniel 6:23–24)

52 God was glorified in a pagan nation because of the three Hebrew children's ____ in Him (Daniel 3:28)

56 When those who were bitten would ____ at the serpent on the pole, they would be healed (Numbers 21:8)

57 "But what ____ we, that you complain against us?" (Exodus 16:7)

58 God ordained the ____ of Unleavened Bread to be observed throughout future generations (Exodus 12:17)

59 Time and again God miraculously delivered His people, the children of ____ (Exodus 3:10)

61 "We have ____, for we have spoken against the LORD and against you" (Numbers 21:7)

62 At Horeb, water came out of the rock after Moses ____ it (Exodus 17:6)

66 The furnace was exceedingly ____ (Daniel 3:22)

67 "Now the blood shall be a ____ for you" (Exodus 12:13)

68 The king ordered his army to ____ the three Hebrew children (Daniel 3:20)

69 "The flood was ____ the earth forty days" (Genesis 7:17)

70 Daniel continued to ____ as was his custom, despite the king's decree (Daniel 6:10)

73 He helped hold up Moses' hands at Rephidim (Exodus 17:12)

75 "Do what ____ right in His sight" (Exodus 15:26)

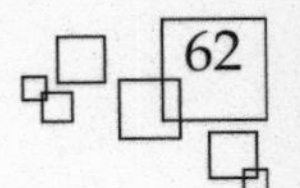

*I*n Acts 2:5 we read about how "there were dwelling in Jerusalem Jews, devout men, from every nation under heaven." The chapter goes on to list fifteen nations or regions from which these men came. These men heard the gospel spoken in their own lanuages on the day of Pentecost. See how many of the fifteen nations or regions you can find in the letter grid below before looking them up in your Bible.

E I G Y H P M S A E G Y L I B C P
D L M E S O A I L O P A D A C O T
E A E E P A I S A B Y A E P N N P
C A D J T P M B L E M A J T B O A
A R O U A E A Y P A G E U I E A R
D A J P S Y T A T Y I S D N T R S
U B U A L G O C M R H P E I U O C
J I D M E L P A R T H I A T A M P
C A P P A D O C I A C R E Y E E A
L I M H I L S O Y S A T B H P L R
Y A A Y B I E R I L J I P C R Y A
H P S L L E M E A C L Y R Y G H P
O E P I J U D B T P G E S I G P A
M M Y A I G Y R H P T O D O S E M

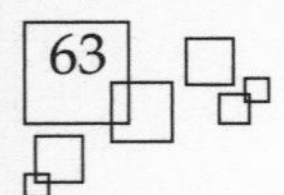

Jesus did not play favorites, but He gave special designations to some of His disciples. John is referred to by an expression we'd all like to have applied to us: "The one whom Jesus loved."

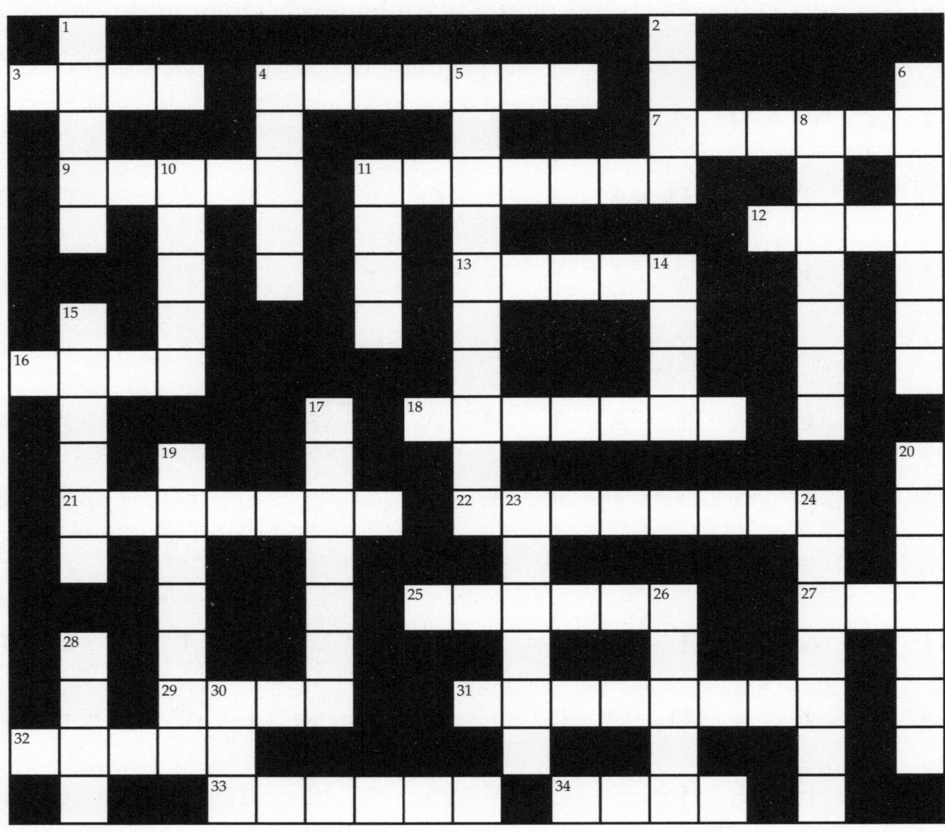

Across

3 Outside the Beautiful Gate, a man asked for these from Peter and John (Acts 3:3)

4 The man carrying this container of water showed Peter and John the Upper Room (Luke 22:10)

7 Sitting opposite this house of worship, His disciples asked questions about the end times (Mark 13:3–4)

9 John and two disciples extended this hand of fellowship to Paul and Barnabas (Galatians 2:9)

11 John was one of these "supporting structures" of the church (Galatians 2:9)

12 Jesus didn't want John and James to command this "flame" from heaven against #24 Down (Luke 9:54)

13 This former sorcerer wanted Peter and John to sell him some of God's power (Acts 8:18–19)

16 The man in #3 Across suffered from this condition

18 On Patmos, John heard a loud voice, sounding like this brass instrument (Revelation 1:10)

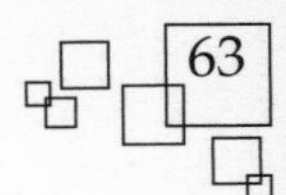

21 John's name is used on three of these (sing.)

22 The man in #4 Across was told that the "Instructor" (pl.) needed his guest room (Luke 22:11)

25 In #7 Across, John, Jesus, and three other disciples were siting on this mount (Mark 13:3)

27 John became a fisher of these (Luke 5:10)

29 "He who has the Son has ____," John wrote (1 John 5:12)

31 In #22 Across, they needed the Upper Room to observe this festival (Luke 22:8)

32 John also wrote, "He who ____ his brother is in darkness" (1 John 2:11)

33 On the cross, Jesus said to the disciple about Mary, His mother, "Behold your ____!" (John 19:27)

34 Peter and John told the Sanhedrin that they had to speak the things they had ____ and heard (Acts 4:20)

Down

1 James and John wanted to sit on either side of Jesus in His "majesty," in heaven (Mark 10:35–37)

2 John was mending one of these when he met Jesus (Matthew 4:21)

4 He was John's partner in missions after the Resurrection (Acts 3:1)

5 #13 Across wanted the ability to give this gift (2 words)—but only God can (Acts 8:18–19)

6 John's father (Matthew 4:21)

8 Peter and John were put into custody by these spiritual leaders, among others (Acts 4:1–3)

10 John, James, and Cephas perceived the "divine mercy" Paul had received, and approved (Galatians 2:9)

11 John, James, and Cephas wanted Paul and Barnabas to remember the "destitute" (Galatians 2:10)

14 Of one through ten, at which hour did Peter and John go to the temple? (Acts 3:1)

15 The man in #4 Across was the "lord" of his house (Luke 22:11)

17 The district where John came from (Matthew 4:18–21)

19 The "act of God" performed for the man in #3 Across put John and Peter in custody

20 Jesus called John and James the "Sons of ____" (Mark 3:17)

23 John and James referred to this prophet in #12 Across (Luke 9:54)

24 A village in this region rejected Jesus; John and James wanted to see it consumed (Luke 9:51–54)

26 Jesus said that not one "rock" would be left upon another in the end times (Mark 13:2)

28 John used this vessel in his former profession (Matthew 4:21)

30 Suffix meaning a doctrine or theory

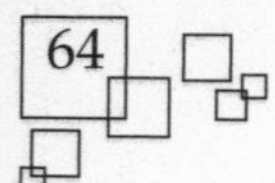

*H*ow would *you* interpret these strange markings if they appeared on a wall while you were attending a king's banquet?

See Daniel 5:25 if you get stumped.

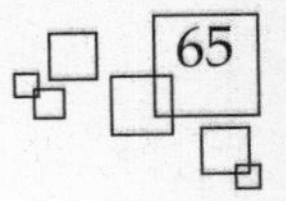

*P*RISON GUIDE

Throughout the Scriptures we find angels performing some very special tasks for God. Sometimes they were tasks of a miraculous nature. Angels were sent to shut the lions' mouths against Daniel, to release Peter from prison, and to accompany the children of Israel as they crossed the Red Sea. At other times, angels appeared to change the direction a person was going. Balaam didn't see the angel his donkey saw that was sent to thwart Balaam's wicked purposes. Jacob wrestled all night with an angel and become lame from the struggle.

In most cases these beings probably didn't look anything like the traditional image of a winged figure with a halo. Indeed, we know that at least a few of them were mistaken for ordinary people until the extraordinary occurred. The angels that visited with Abraham dined and lodged with his family before they went to Sodom to warn Lot of the city's doom.

Begin at the right arm of the cross and end up back on the left arm of the cross on the angel's face.

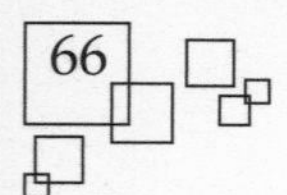

Connect the blocks below, which are based on a previous puzzle, to reveal the meaning of the message that appeared on King Belshazzar's wall during a feast in which he used the sacred vessels from the temple in Jerusalem. (See Daniel 5.)

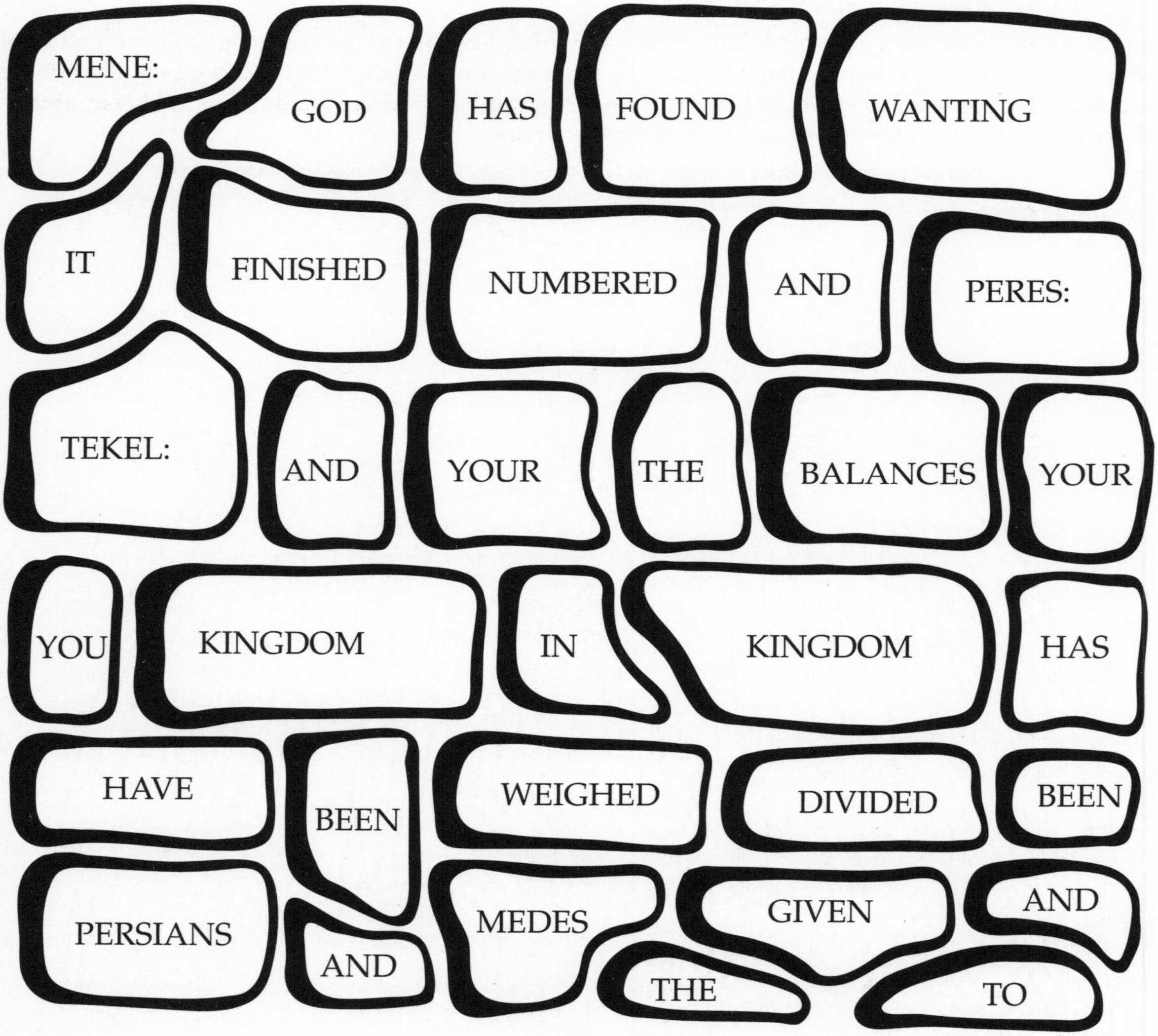

MENE: GOD HAS FOUND WANTING

IT FINISHED NUMBERED AND PERES:

TEKEL: AND YOUR THE BALANCES YOUR

YOU KINGDOM IN KINGDOM HAS

HAVE BEEN WEIGHED DIVIDED BEEN

PERSIANS AND MEDES THE GIVEN AND TO

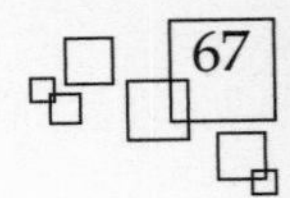

*E*arly Christians endured a lot more of this than modern-day Christians have.

Clue: MESSIAH *is* JTNNSFV

W Q T N N T G   F Y T   B V X N T

A V X   F Y T   O T Y N T U Z B T G

E X Y   Y S H V B T X Z N P T N N,

N F R T,   E X Y   B V T S Y N

S N   B V T   R S P H G X J

X E   V T F M T P.

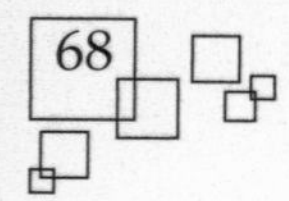

THE SEVEN-POINTED STAR

This star shape is also called the Mystic Star. It is an emblem that represents the sevenfold Spirit of God—seven being the biblical number for the perfection of God. In Revelation 3:1 we see the probable origin for this emblem: "These things says He who has the seven Spirits of God and the seven stars." Jesus Christ was frequently referred to by early Christians as the "Bright and Morning Star"—One who was fully aglow with the spirt of God. (See Revelation 22:16.)

When used as a church-related emblem, the star is red (flame color) to signify the penetrating, all-consuming power of God's spirit.

Start →

↖ End

*T*he story of Ruth in the Bible is a tragic story that has a happy ending. Some of the words in the crossword are from the book of Ruth.

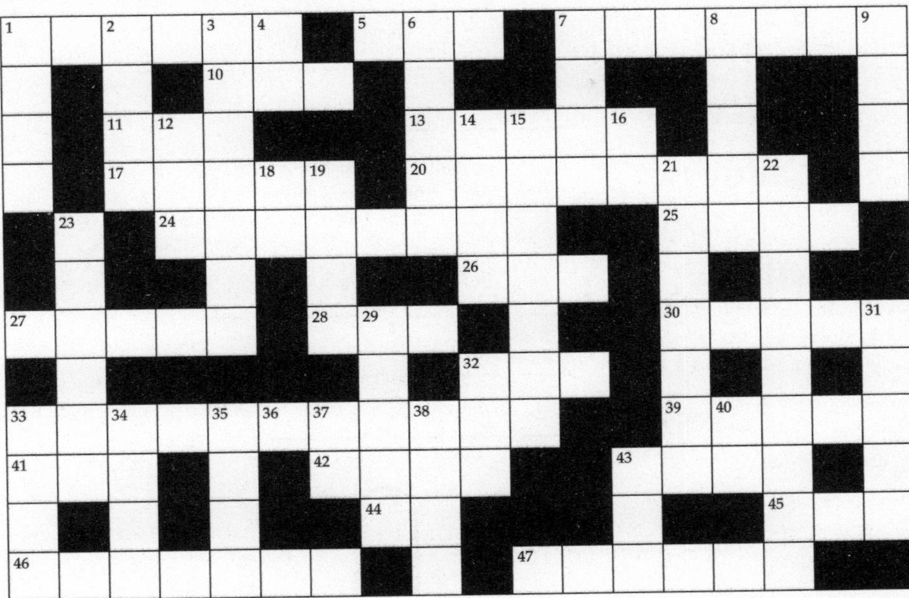

Across

1 Grain Ruth gathered (Ruth 2:17)
5 Before two
7 Boaz told the worker to allow her to work among these (Ruth 2:7)
10 Mesh or profit
11 Vietnamese holiday
13 Ruth's sister-in-law (Ruth 1:4)
17 Concubines and all
20 Union
24 Boaz to Naomi
25 "Ask not for whom the ____ #39 Across"
26 First lady
27 Love, a matter of the ____
28 Dined
30 Tree parts
32 Affirmative
33 Naomi to Ruth (3 words) (Ruth 1:14)
39 "Ask not for whom the #25 Across ____"
41 Mouths
42 Obtained by force
43 Ancient stringed instrument
44 Camper (abbr.)
45 Demure
46 Equilibrium
47 Sanctuary

Down

1 Ruth's beloved
2 Boaz's beloved
3 "____ me not to leave you" (Ruth 1:16)
4 King James "you"
6 Person Ruth would not leave (Ruth 1:22)
7 Luminary
8 Saying
9 "You are the ____ of the earth" (Matthew 5:13)
12 "He who has an ____, let him hear what the Spirit says" (Revelation 2:7)
14 Rant's partner
15 See ahead of time
16 Slang greeting
18 Spanish "the"
19 Name Naomi called herself because of her grief (Ruth 1:20)
21 Skill
22 Naomi's husband and Boaz's family name (Ruth 1:2; 2:1)
23 Shaking
29 Male voice
31 Impudent or cheeky
32 Asian ox
33 Country of Ruth's birth (Ruth 1:4)
34 Short's opposite
35 Equal
37 Third person, neuter
38 Ruth's motivation (Ruth 4:15)
40 Either's partner
43 Nickname for Louis

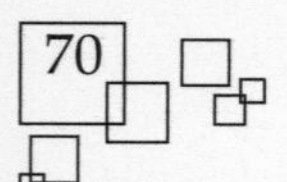

*U*nscramble the names of these seven key Bible figures and place them in the grid below to reveal a response they all had in common.

HRABAAM ___ ___ ___ ___ ___ ___ ___

SEUA ___ ___ ___ ___

BCOJA ___ ___ ___ ___ ___

ASELUM ___ ___ ___ ___ ___ ___

JEPSOH ___ ___ ___ ___ ___ ___

SAAIIH ___ ___ ___ ___ ___ ___

SOMSE ___ ___ ___ ___ ___

1. ___ ___ ___ ___ ___ ___

2. ___ ___ ___ ___

3. ___ ___ ___ ___ ___ ___ ___

4. ___ ___ ___ ___ ___ ___

5. ___ ___ ___ ___ ___ ___

6. ___ ___ ___ ___ ___

7. ___ ___ ___ ___ ___

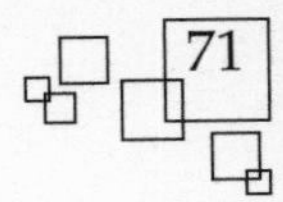

Some things are too HOT to handle!

Find eleven items in the letter grid below that the Bible describes as being HOT. (See how many you can find before consulting the Scripture Pool.)

O	N	A	N	G	E	P	O	A	L	S	T	D
R	F	O	P	O	V	E	N	S	I	D	O	I
I	U	T	H	S	I	D	P	O	A	O	N	S
A	R	I	O	E	T	A	S	L	R	U	P	P
E	E	R	U	S	A	E	L	P	S	I	D	L
H	B	S	T	N	S	R	N	H	T	C	I	C
E	E	R	G	G	T	B	T	O	R	O	R	O
V	A	E	E	N	R	O	R	T	E	A	P	A
O	R	S	M	A	E	I	S	L	A	O	C	H
A	E	C	A	N	R	U	F	C	M	L	S	E
R	G	L	P	S	I	D	A	O	S	V	O	A
B	E	R	T	S	N	R	U	F	R	T	S	P

Scripture Pool

EXODUS 16:21 DEUTERONOMY 9:19 DEUTERONOMY 19:6 JOSHUA 9:12 JOB 6:15–17
PSALM 39:3 PROVERBS 6:28 EZEKIEL 24:11 DANIEL 3:22
HOSEA 7:7 1 TIMOTHY 4:2

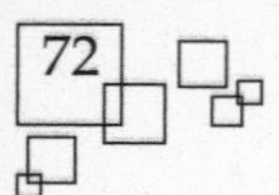

*M*ost of the words in this crossword begin with the letter "S."

Across

1 Abram's wife (Genesis 12:5)

4 Jonah was cast into the heart of it (pl.) (Jonah 2:3)

7 The Lord told Moses, "____ the laver between the tabernacle of meeting and the altar" (Exodus 40:7)

9 Isaiah said we all have gone astray like ____ (Isaiah 53:6)

10 God said, "Let there ____ light" (Genesis 1:3)

12 As priest of Israel, he anointed both Saul and David to be kings (1 Samuel 10:1; 16:13)

14 Isaac's mother (Genesis 21:1–3)

17 Neither, nor; either, ____

18 Jesus sent out His disciples with only a staff, one tunic, and their ____ (Mark 6:7–9)

21 A prophet was formerly called this (1 Samuel 9:9)

22 Deep sadness

23 Bashful

25 Chief of the evil spirits

26 Stigmata

29 Emergency signal, literally meaning "save our souls"

32 The king asked Nehemiah, "Why is your face ____?" (Nehemiah 2:2)

33 Israel offered these at Beersheba (Genesis 46:1)

35 Behold, in Old English

36 A Jewish chief priest in Ephesus, his seven sons were attacked by an evil spirit (Acts 19:13–16)

37 The psalmist prayed, "Uphold my steps in Your paths, that my footsteps may not ____" (Psalm 17:5)

39 We are always to test them to see if they are of God (1 John 4:1)

41 Day of rest

43 Jesus' final words on the cross were, "____ is finished" (John 19:30)

45 Lot's wife became a pillar of this (Genesis 19:15, 26)

46 Paul taught that the wages for these is death (Romans 6:23)

47 Jesus asked, "How can one . . . plunder his goods, unless he first binds the ____ ____?" (2 words) (Matthew 12:29)

49 Jonathan loved David "as his own ____" (1 Samuel 18:1)

50 After ascension (abbr.)

52 Daniel was called by the king, "____ of the living God" (Daniel 6:20)

54 Esau was called this, which literally means "red" (Genesis 25:30)

55 Eli fell off one backwards and died when he heard that the ark of God had been captured (1 Samuel 4:11–18)

57 Open-palmed blow to the face

58 He killed more enemy Philistines at the time of his death than in his entire life (Judge 16:30)

60 Jesus referred to Himself mostly as "the ____ of man"

61 John heard the Lord's voice as "the ____ of many waters" (Revelation 1:15)

62 The shaft of Goliath's was like a weaver's beam (2 Samuel 21:19)

63 Judas's kiss was one (2 words) (Matthew 26:48)

Down

1 Cry

2 Isaiah prophesied a highway from Egypt to here (Isaiah 19:23)

3 Jesus taught, "No one, when he has lit a lamp, puts it in ____ ____ place" (2 words) (Luke 11:33)

4 Sign to the wise men that a new King had been born

5 Paul wrote that to Abraham, circumcision was a "____ of the righteousness" of his faith (Romans 4:11)

6 Moses sent twelve men into Canaan to do this (Numbers 13:17)

8 Name of altar built by Jacob: ____ Bethel (Genesis 35:7)

9 Earth

11 Organ of seeing

13 Señora

14 What a sower goes out to do (Matthew 13:3)

15 Residue of a fire

16 Straw

19 He had an army of 580,000 men of valor, yet cried to the Lord, "We rest on You" (2 Chronicles 14:8, 11)

20 Color of sins before they are made white as snow (Isaiah 1:18)

24 Jesus said He was sent, "____ God so loved the world" (John 3:16)

26 First king of Israel

27 Certificate of Deposit (abbr.)

28 Mourning garment

29 Jesus said they sit with the Pharisees in Moses' seat and "they say, and do not do" (Matthew 23:2–3)

30 Paul taught we are reconciled by Jesus to be "holy, and blameless, and above reproach in His ____" (Colossians 1:22)

31 It was sent into the wilderness once a year as part of the atonement (Leviticus 16:6–10)

33 Jesus sent His disciples to be witnesses to "Jerusalem, and in all Judea and ____, and to the end of the earth" (Acts 1:8)

34 Moses commanded them not to be mistreated (Exodus 22:21)

38 David asked Saul's soldiers, "____ there not a cause?" (1 Samuel 17:29)

40 The Levites cried, "____ up and bless the Lord" (Nehemiah 9:5)

42 Sweltering

44 The number of men hidden by Rahab (Joshua 2:4)

45 Temple builder known for his great wisdom

47 Joseph told his brothers, "God sent me before you . . . to ____ your lives by a great deliverance" (Genesis 45:7)

48 The Son of man gave His life as one (Mark 10:45)

49 Prerequisite for harvests; given to sower by the Lord (pl.) (Isaiah 55:10)

51 A woman with a flow of blood only wanted to touch this part of Jesus' garment (Matthew 9:20)

52 Paul said, "As the truth of Christ is in me, no one shall ____ me from this boasting" (2 Corinthians 11:10)

53 The Lord said the morning stars did this as He laid the cornerstone of the earth (Job 38:6–7)

55 The trees of the Lord are full of it (Psalm 104:16)

56 A donkey; Balaam's spoke to him (Numbers 22:30, KJV)

59 Direction of Syria from Israel

Now unscramble the circled letters in the grid to reveal one of the foremost symbolic figures in the Bible:

___ ___ ___ ___ ___ ___ ___ ___ ___ ___ ___ ___

(2 words)

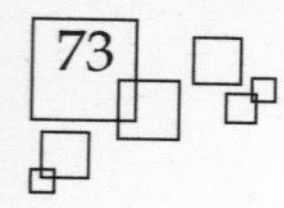

*E*SCAPE FROM *P*HARAOH

*H*aving been raised in an Egyptian household as the adopted grandson of the Pharaoh, Moses nevertheless was very aware of his Israelite heritage and eventually became very resentful of the slavery of his people.

One day Moses observed an Israelite slave being beaten. Moses' anger overcame him and he killed the Egyptian oppressor. This sealed his fate with Pharaoh, who would have had Moses put to death if he could have been apprehended. But Moses fled for his life. He left Egypt, headed into the Midian desert, and became a sheepherder. Forty years later, Moses returned to Egypt at God's direction to free the Israelites from slavery.

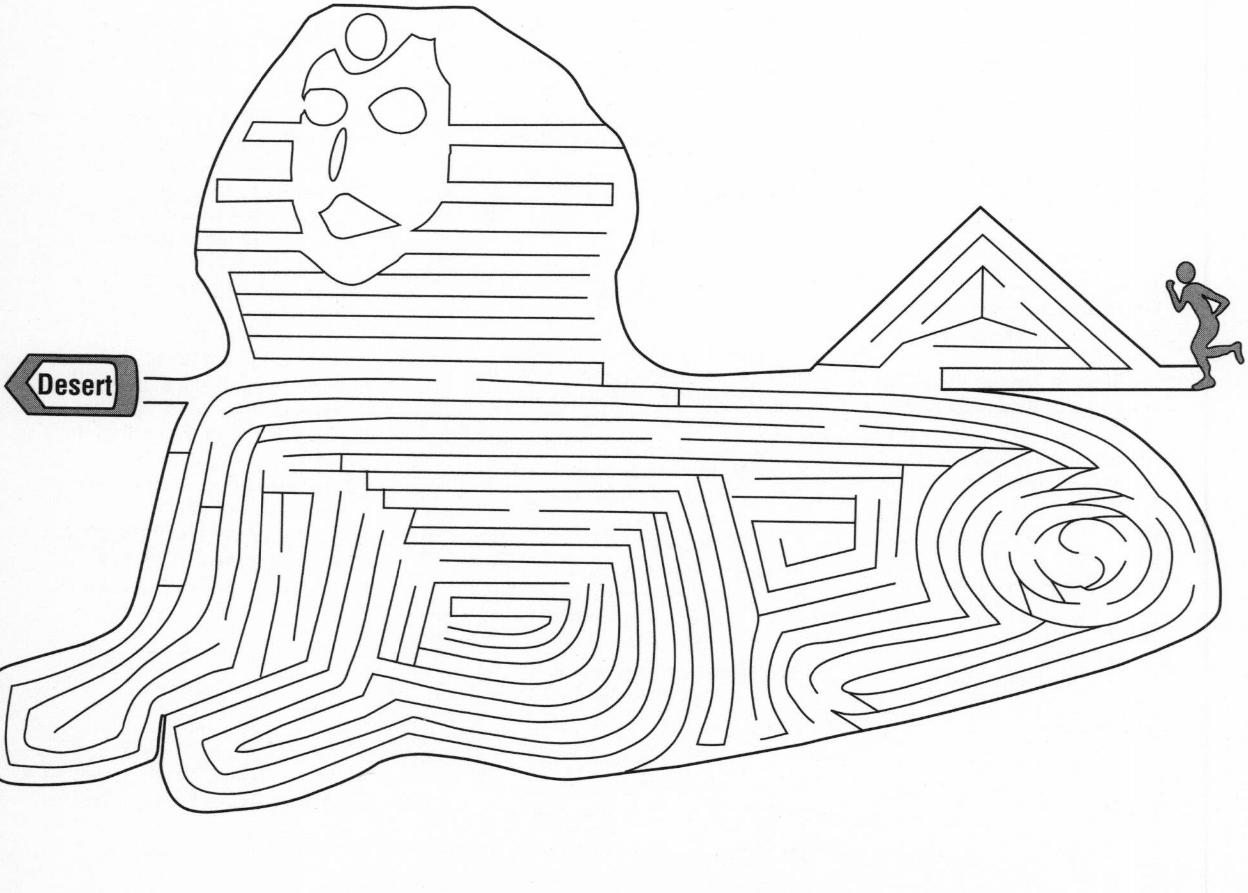

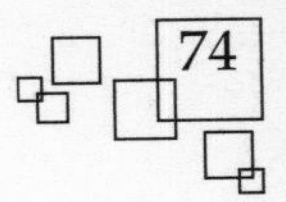

*H*ot on the heels of the previous puzzle. . .

Clue: **MESSIAH** *is* **SSIAHME**

N OWYO URWO RKSTH'

ATYO UAR ENE ITHERCO

LDNO RHO TIC. O ULDWI

SHYO UWE RECO LDORHO

TSO. TH ENBE' CAUSEYO

UAR ELU KEWARMAN' DNE

ITHERCO LDNO RHO TIW'

I LLVO MITYO UOU TOF MY

MO UTHRE. VELATIONIK 3:15–16

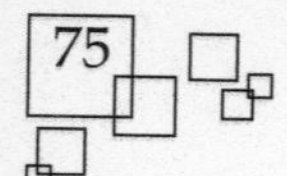

*T*he magnificent magnificat! Fill in as many of the words as you can from Mary's great praise song without consulting Luke 1:46–55.

And Mary said:

________ (36 down) ________ (24 Across) ________ (14 Across) the ________ (48 Across), and my ________ (22 Across) has rejoiced in ________ (39 Down)

my ________ (11 Down). For ________ (34 Across) has regared the lowly ________ (25 Down) of ________ (34 Down) ________ (37 Across); ________ (45 Down)

behold, henceforth ________ (8 Across) ________ (7 Down) will ________ (31 Across) me ________ (43 Across). For He who is ________ (18 Across)

has done ________ (7 Across) ________ (3 Across) for ________ (36 Across), and ________ (4 Down) is His ________ (28 Down). And His ________ (26 Down)

is on those who ________ (42 Down) ________ (44 Across) ________ (49 Across) generation to generation. He has ________ (5 Down)

________ (27 Across) with His ________ (40 Down); He has ________ (21 Down) the ________ (16 Down) in the ________ (23 Across) ________ (47 Down)

their ________ (20 Across). He has ________ (19 Across) ________ (10 Across) the mighty from their ________ (46 Across), and ________ (2 Down)

the ________ (6 Down). He has ________ (29 Down) the ________ (38 Across) with ________ (9 Across) things, and the ________ (33 Down) He

has ________ (41 Down) away ________ (15 Across). He has ________ (35 Down) His ________ (24 Down) ________ (1 Across), in ________ (32 Across)

of His ________ (26 Down), as He ________ (12 Down) to ________ (17 Across) ________ (29 Across), to ________ (13 Down) and to ________ (44 Down)

________ (30 Down) ________ (45 Across).

UPPER ROOM

In remembering the Last Supper, we sometimes forget that the event was actually part of the Passover feast celebrated by all Jews. As recounted in Mark 14, Jesus' disciples were virtually blind to the real significance of the events of that week. The scribes were plotting to kill Jesus, but the fact that it was a holy week prevented them from carrying out their plans. A woman, having anointed Jesus' feet with expensive perfume, was severely criticized for the seeming waste of the costly oils. But Jesus described what she did as His anointing for burial.

Later the disciples inquired as to where Jesus might wish to celebrate the Passover feast. Jesus instructed them to go to a certain house where they were shown a large upper room, furnished and prepared for guests where they were to make ready the feast, which became the Last Supper.

End

Start

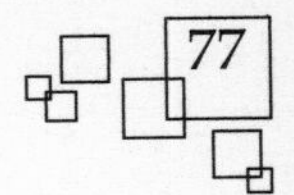

*T*he reality of hell is the same for everyone. From the clues and scriptures below, find twenty words that are hidden in the letter box that tell us something about a place we want to avoid.

O N L I E N Y O I S C O R P I O N S H O T

H I N Y L C S D E W L A W L E S S M O E T

G R T E H P O R P E S L A F N H O E U W Y

N O H I I L O R M E N G A E O D D U N O R

I P R S A J I O X P D O R L F O E N B P A

K E W T N E M H S I N U P B O R K O E Q C

E R E O T S N J M N O T Q A H I C R L P S

E R N O P O N O T G R E E N O P I H I A C

S C C O I R P O N L K R O I Q F W O E D Z

F N O I T C U R T S E D O M F Y R O V E T

L A W O O E Z S W C U A O O B O I B I A E

E G A O O R I G N A S R E B L O E P N T W

S O R R Y E O N N L Q K O A P A O S G H O

E I D T S R A I L O A N O P S Q R O N G E

E E L O L S A H E L L E A T S I N O O G B

E A Y I D O L S O P R S W I T C H E M O P

R E V I L P R A T O E S R E R E D R U M T

B E T E O Q T N E M R O T W I T H O U T I

D C U R S E D G H Y P O C R I T E S W O E

What hell is like:

Matthew 8:12; Revelation 19:20; Matthew 25:46; 2 Thessalonians 1:9

Who will be there:

Psalm 9:17; Matthew 25:41; Romans 2:8; Revelation 19:20; Revelation 21:8

What will happen there:

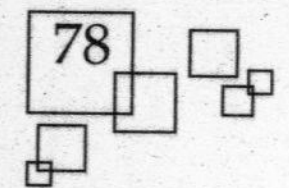

*B*elow is the family tree of Abraham—his sons and grandsons by his wife, Sarah; his wife's servant Hagar; and his second wife Keturah.

Use these names to fill in the crossword grid on the next page.

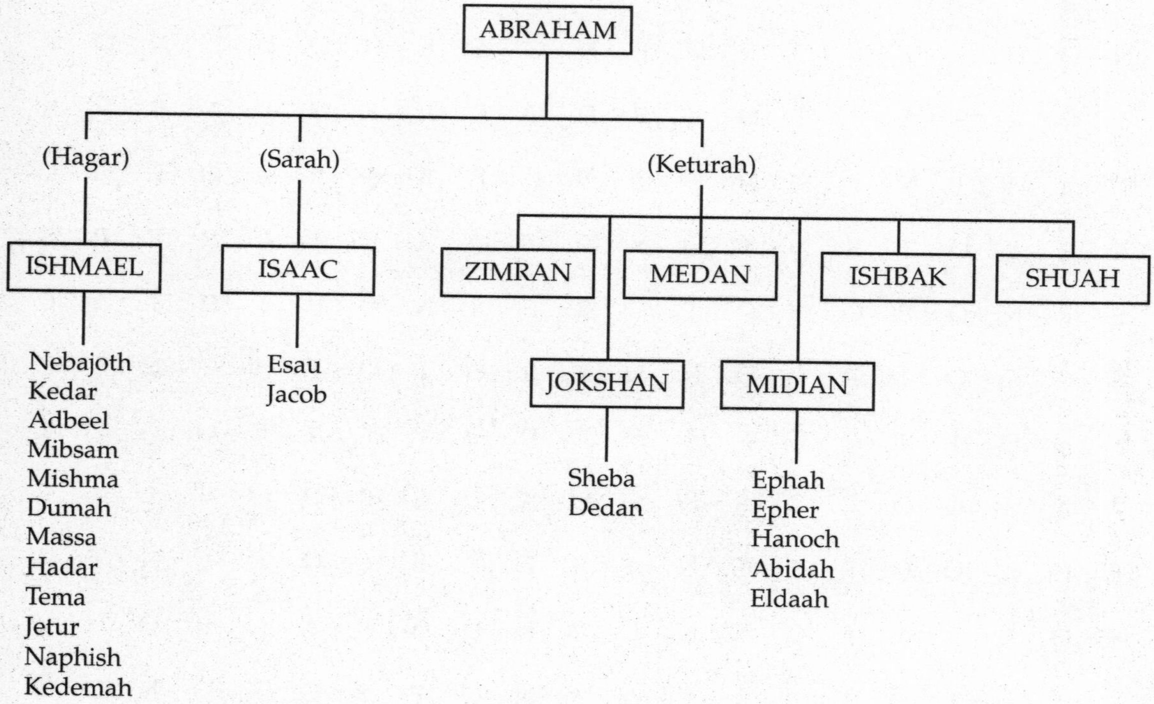

- ABRAHAM
  - (Hagar)
    - ISHMAEL
      - Nebajoth
      - Kedar
      - Adbeel
      - Mibsam
      - Mishma
      - Dumah
      - Massa
      - Hadar
      - Tema
      - Jetur
      - Naphish
      - Kedemah
  - (Sarah)
    - ISAAC
      - Esau
      - Jacob
  - (Keturah)
    - ZIMRAN
    - JOKSHAN
      - Sheba
      - Dedan
    - MEDAN
    - MIDIAN
      - Ephah
      - Epher
      - Hanoch
      - Abidah
      - Eldaah
    - ISHBAK
    - SHUAH

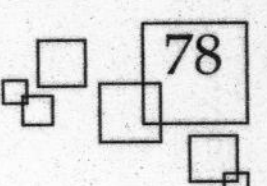

Across
1 Keturah's fifth son
3 Ishmael's tenth son
6 Ishmael's ninth son
7 Abraham's only son by Sarah
8 Keturah's third son
11 Ishmael's eleventh son
12 Midian's fourth son
14 Midian's second son
15 Jokshan's second son
16 Midian's first son
17 Ishmael's fourth son
21 Ishmael's twelfth son
22 Ishmael's fifth son
23 Ishmael's eight son

Down
2 Jokshan's first son
3 Keturah's second son
4 Isaac's firstborn twin
5 Isaac's secondborn twin
7 Abraham's only son by Hagar
8 Keturah's fourth son
9 Ishmael's first son
10 Keturah's first son
12 Ishmael's third son
13 Midian's third son
15 Ishmael's sixth son
16 Midian's fifth son
18 Keturah's sixth son
19 Ishmael's seventh son
20 Ishmael's second son

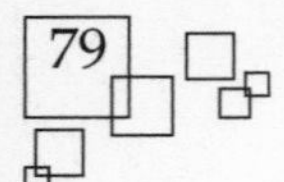

*T*he Church is not intended to be a destination point but a place a refuge, solace, training, and inspiration as we come and go from it as the Lord's witnesses in the world.

End

Start

SEVEN YEARS TO RACHEL

The story of Jacob and Rachel, found in Genesis 29, is one of the great love stories of the Bible. After Jacob tricked his father, Isaac, into giving him the family blessing, Jacob fled from his angry brother, Esau, to take refuge with his uncle Laban. There, Jacob met and fell hopelessly in love with Laban's younger daughter, Rachel. Laban agreed to let Jacob marry Rachel in exchange for seven years of labor. So in love was Jacob that the years "seemed but a few days to him because of the love he had for her" (v. 20). But Laban tricked Jacob. Finding it necessary to marry off the elder daughter, Leah, before Rachel could marry, Laban allowed Jacob to wed Leah thinking she was Rachel. Eventually, Jacob was to marry his beloved Rachel, but not before Laban had extracted seven *more* years of labor for permission to marry her.

Jacob followed his heart through seven years of labor for Rachel. For Jacob to get to Rachel, go once through each of the seven grid boxes, but do not cross any lines without a heart.

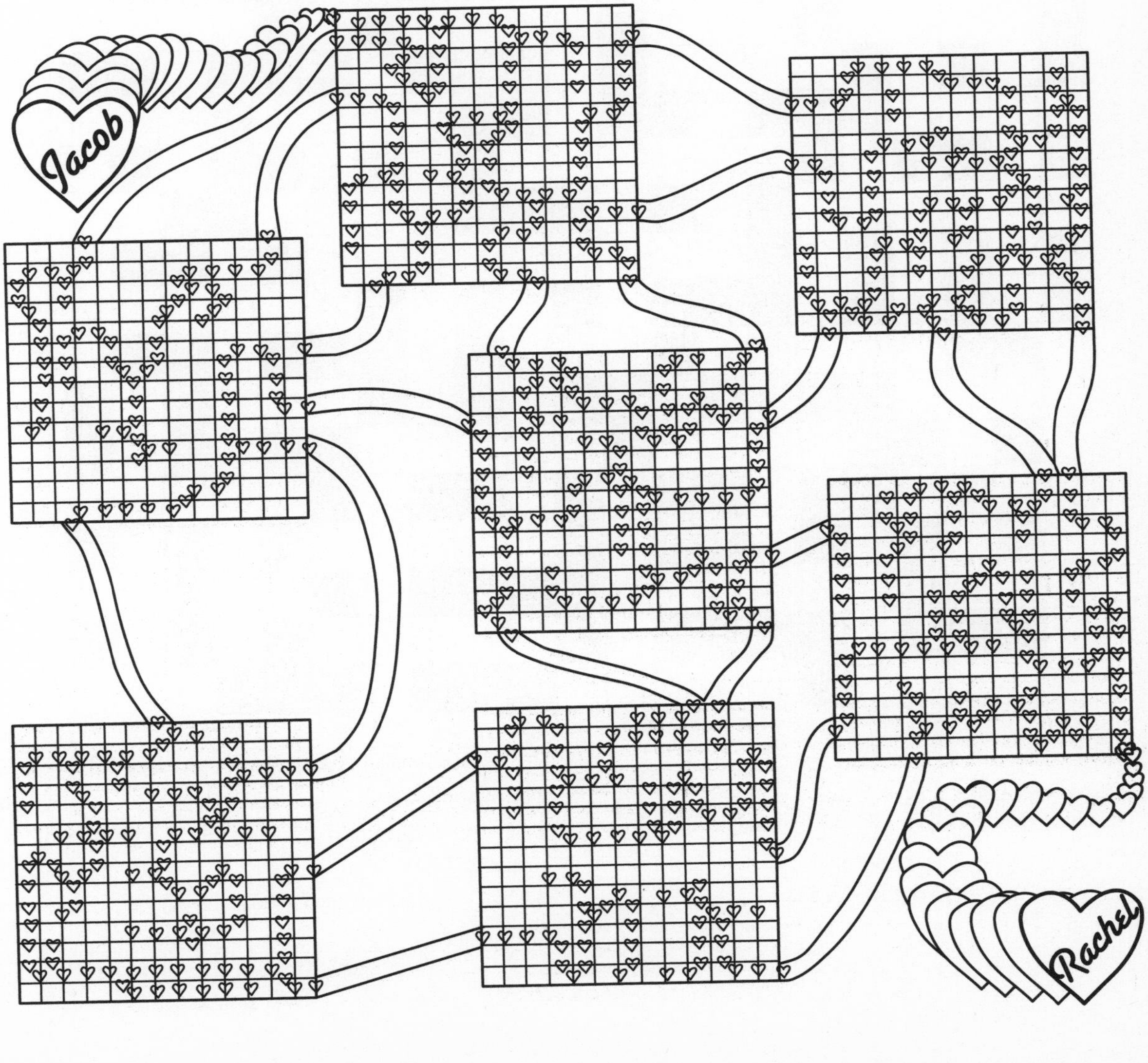

Jacob

Rachel

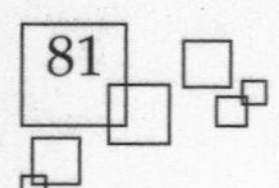

*L*ost . . . and found. In Luke 15 Jesus tells about three things that were lost and then found. Most of the answers for this crossword come from that chapter.

Across

1 Man's response who found his lost sheep (Luke 15:5)

5 "Your brother was dead and ____ alive again" (Luke 15:32)

7 The son who became angry (Luke 15:25)

11 Compensate

12 "I am no longer worthy to be____ your son" (Luke 15:19)

13 The ____ and nine (Luke 15:4, KJV)

16 Nourishment

17 The brother's complaint: "I ____ transgressed your commandment; . . . yet you ____ gave me a young goat" (Luke 15:29)

18 The younger son asked for his "allotment" of his inheritance (Luke 15:12)

20 Swine food (Luke 15:16)

24 Search (Luke 15:8, KJV)

25 See (past tense) (Luke 15:20)

26 Female spouse

27 Jesus said, "A certain man had two ____ " (Luke 15:11)

28 The shepherd, the woman, and the father each had something of value "disappear" (Luke 15:4, 8, 24)

30 Greater (Luke 15:7)

31 Opposite of alive (Luke 15:32)

33 At this moment (Luke 15:25)

36 The father expressed his affection to his son in this way (Luke 15:20)

38 Male parent (Luke 15:12)

41 Null and ____

42 "____ what woman" (Luke 15:8)

43 "Friends and ____ " (Luke 15:6, 9)

46 Sufficient (Luke 15:17)

48 The prodigal's confession: "I have sinned against heaven and in your ____ " (Luke 15:21)

50 "Distant" country (Luke 15:13)

51 The father ordered the servants to "bring out the best ____" (Luke 15:22)

54 Yours and mine

56 "He began to be in ____ " (Luke 15:14)

57 Possessions (Luke 15:12)

59 Ceased living

61 When the son came home "they began to be ____ " (Luke 15:24)

63 "Safe and ____" (Luke 15:27)

64 Supreme being

65 Starvation (Luke 15:17)

66 "Rejoice with ____" (Luke 15:6, 9)

67 ____ merry; ____glad (Luke 15:24, 32)

68 A man who lost one of these searched until he found it (Luke 15:4)

69 "____ a lamp . . . and search carefully until she finds it" (Luke 15:8)

70 Discovers (Luke 15:4, 8)

71 The woman originally had ____ pieces of silver (Luke 15:8)

Down

1 To feel remorse and change your mind (Luke 15:7, 10)

2 Happiness (Luke 15:7)

3 Young cow (Luke 15:23)

4 "It was right that we should . . . be ____ " (Luke 15:32)

6 Brush clean (Luke 15:8)

7 "When he has found it, he lays it ____ his shoulders, rejoicing" (Luke 15:5)

8 The son's homecoming was celebrated with "music and ____ " (Luke 15:25)

9 Dashed (Luke 15:20)

10 The father's invitation to celebrate: "Let us ____ and be merry" (Luke 15:23)

12 The father's "mercy" (Luke 15:20)

14 "All #62 Down I have is____" (Luke 15:31)

15 The ____ famine meant there was not enough food (Luke 15:14)

19 Opposite of on (Luke 15:20)

21 To be in debt

22 Pigs (Luke 15:15)

23 Valuable items that the woman lost (Luke 15:8)

24 The prodigal son's was empty (Luke 15:16)

25 "____ he divided to them his livelihood" (Luke 15:12)

29 You (old English)

31 Wasted; consumed (Luke 15:30)

32 "I will ____ and go to my father" (Luke 15:18)

34 Having value (Luke 15:19)

35 " ____ came to himself"(Luke 15:17)

37 Rigid

39 The woman searched through her "dwelling" to find what was lost (Luke 15:8)

40 Jewelry to wear on a finger (Luke 15:22)

44 Prostitutes (Luke 15:30)

45 Traveled (Luke 15:13)

47 Playboy (Luke 15:13)

49 Where angels rejoice when sinners repent (Luke 15:7)

52 His father's servants had an adequate supply of this, but the son was without (Luke 15:17)

53 If she loses one coin, searches carefully "until she finds ____ ?" (Luke 5:8)

55 Object lesson (Luke 15:3)

58 One who sins (Luke 15:7)

60 Employed (Luke 15:17)

62 "All ____ I have is #14 Down" (Luke 15:31)

*H*ope and healing for God's people.

Clue: MESSIAH *is* NFZZTVA

T R N U B F Q B E F M A Q V K F

G V E E F L P U N U W V N F M T E E

A C N P E F J A F N Z F E I F Z' V W L

B K V U V W L Z F F X N U R V G F'

V W L J C K W R K Q N J A F T K

M T G X F L M V U Z' J A F W T M T E E

A F V K R K Q N A F V I F W' V W L

M T E E R Q K O T I F J A F T K Z T W

V W L A F V E J A F T K E V W L.

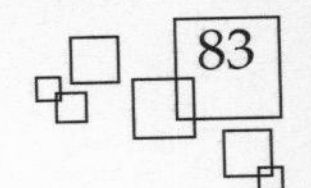

*A*lthough not commonly recognized, the Bible is a book in which laughter and joy are abundant!

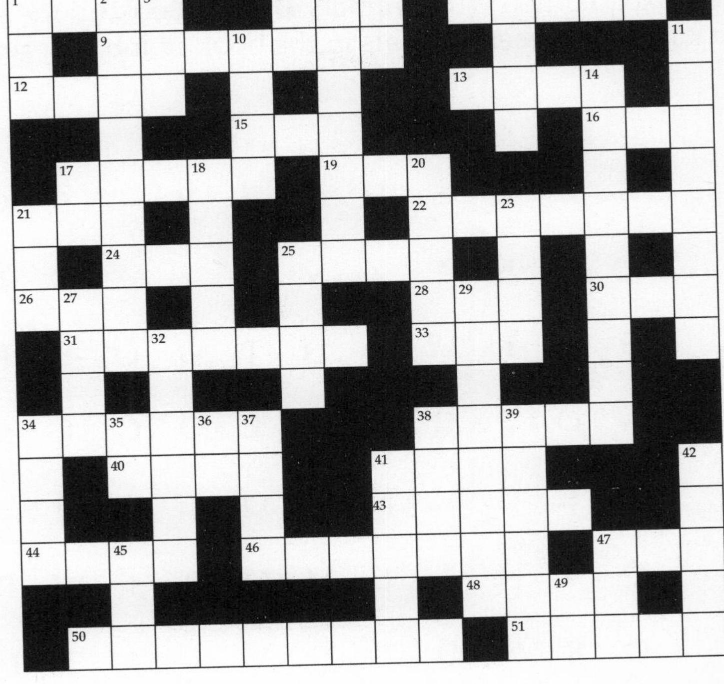

Across

1 Colored
4 Verb of being
7 Grin
9 Giggled
12 Silly smile
13 He made Ruth smile
15 Gone by
16 Everyone
17 He danced for joy before the Lord (2 Samuel 6:14)
19 Sacred initials on a communion table
21 God was not laughing at him in spite of what this man said (Job 9:23)
22 He laughed at the incredible word of the Lord (Genesis 17:17)
24 Ms. Peron
25 Some people will shed one when they laugh OR when they cry
26 Still
28 Pie ____ mode
30 Destruction caused from dampness
31 Chortle
33 Between waist and thigh
34 Evening meal
38 John the Baptist immersed Him (Matthew 3:13)
40 Money/goods exchange
41 Alone
43 Swing around
44 Doe's mate
46 Teacher of sorts
47 Happy's opposite
48 Boulder
50 Pleasured
51 Between shoulders and hips

Down

1 Embrace
2 News of Mary's expectation gave her joy (Luke 1:42)
3 One of Jacob's boys (1 Chronicles 2:1–2)
4 Sound of pleasure
5 Take great joy
6 Short for editor
8 Night light
10 Happy
11 "I will laugh at your ____" (Proverbs 1:26)
14 He rejoiced at the naming of his son, John (Luke 1:63–64)
17 With I, a phrase for bride and groom
18 His parents laughed at the thought he could even be born (Genesis 17:17; 18:12)
20 Mom's name (see #18 Down) (Genesis 17:19)
21 Happiness
23 This comes only if you sow
25 Informed
27 Tannish-white color
29 More full of energy
32 Empty the suitcase
34 Hunk or slice
35 Letter's end
36 Spanish article
37 Remainder
38 He leaped for joy in his mother's womb (Luke 1:41)
39 "____ is better than laughter" (Ecclesiastes 7:3)
41 Jesus sent demons into them (Mark 5:12–13)
42 Former (modern) Egyptian ruler
45 Performer's signal
47 Travel by skimming across the top
49 Big Sur state (abbr.)

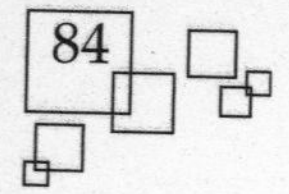

*N*oah is well-known for his floating menagerie, but another Old Testament character is well acquainted with animals as well. Look up the scriptures if you need to, to find the names of fifteen animals in the book of Job.

B	I	O	S	H	C	I	R	T	S	O	P	N	A	X	R
Q	P	N	L	X	M	G	I	A	O	P	N	W	O	A	R
S	I	K	W	A	H	T	O	O	L	R	A	D	N	P	R
N	O	P	Q	A	T	L	O	G	L	D	L	N	O	P	Y
R	E	G	A	N	O	O	I	N	Q	I	N	O	P	E	R
O	S	N	K	L	M	O	P	I	W	R	O	I	K	A	N
O	R	N	Q	L	E	V	I	A	T	H	A	N	C	A	N
S	O	K	N	W	H	O	X	T	R	U	O	S	B	L	E
N	H	Y	E	T	E	K	U	N	A	D	E	E	R	Q	A
J	K	N	W	A	B	O	R	U	P	T	E	B	A	S	U
Q	N	L	G	O	E	Q	A	O	N	K	L	P	V	K	L
O	I	L	O	C	U	S	T	M	T	R	E	N	E	O	I
S	E	N	O	M	K	L	P	Q	A	S	E	G	N	E	D

Scripture Pool

JOB 38:39, 41; 39:1, 5, 9, 13, 19–20, 26–27; 40:15; 41:1

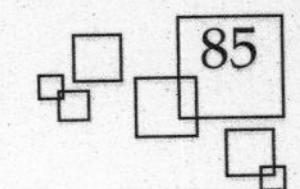

*A*fter the multitude left, the disciples asked Jesus to explain the parable of the wheat and the tares. The words below are some of the words Jesus used in that parable. Fill in the blanks to find Jesus' explanation. Then, using the same code, fill in the blanks for His final word to the twelve.

1. F ___ ___ ___ D is the ___ ___ ___ ___ D

   4 2 5 11 7 8 5

2. G ___ ___ D ___ ___ ___ D ___ are the ___ ___ N ___ ___ F

   7 7 9 2 2 9 9 7 9 7

   ___ ___ ___ K ___ N G D ___ ___

   10 3 2 4 7 6

3. ___ ___ ___ ___ ___ are the ___ ___ N ___ ___ F ___ ___ ___

   10 1 8 2 9 9 7 9 7 10 3 2

   ___ ___ C K ___ D ___ N ___

   11 4 2 7 2

4. ___ N ___ ___ Y is the D ___ V ___ ___

   2 2 6 2 4 5

5. ___ ___ ___ V ___ ___ ___ is the ___ N D ___ F ___ ___ ___ ___ G ___

   3 1 8 2 9 10 2 7 10 3 2 1 2

6. ___ ___ ___ P ___ ___ ___ are the ___ N G ___ ___ ___

   8 2 1 2 8 9 1 2 5 9

Jesus' word of admonition to the disciples:

___ ___ ___ ___ ___ ___ ___ ___

3 2 11 3 7 3 1 9

___ ___ ___ ___ ___ ___ ___ ___ ___ ___,

2 1 8 9 10 7 3 2 1 8

___ ___ ___ ___ ___ ___ ___ ___ ___ ___!

5 2 10 3 4 6 3 2 1 8

Puzzle Answers

1

3

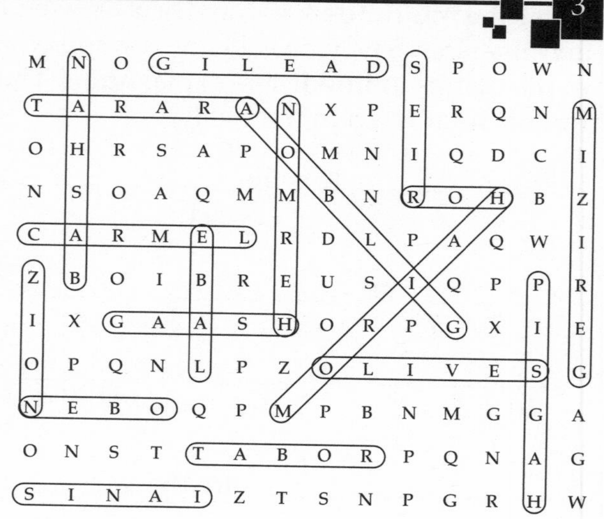

4

Blessed are them meek, for they shall inherit the earth. (Matthew 5:5)

2

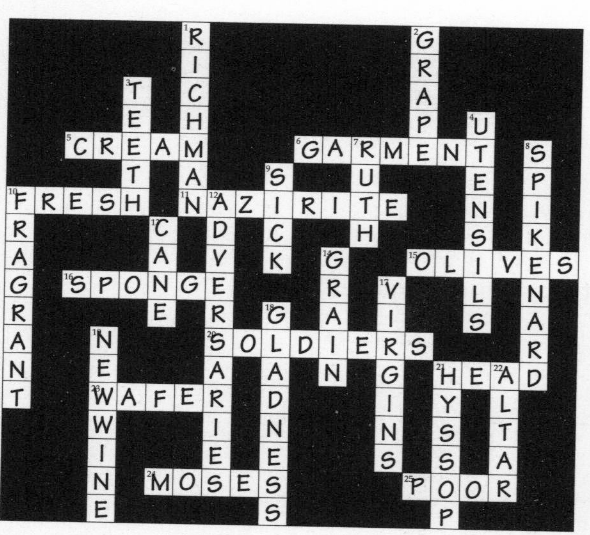

5

6

BANQUET
PURIM
ZERESH
HEGAI
HAMAN
AHASUERUS
GALLOWS
VASHTI
SHUSHAN
FEASTS
MORDECAI

7

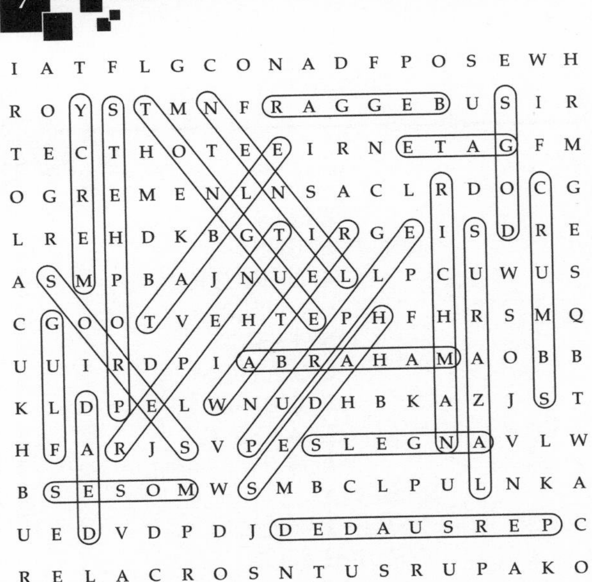

8

9

Puzzle Answers

10

Blessed are those who hunger and thirst for righteousness, for they shall be filled.
(Matthew 5:6)

11

12

I will make you a great nation; I will bless you and make your name great; and you shall be a blessing. I will bless those who bless you, and I will curse him who curses you; and in you all the families of the earth shall be blessed.
(Genesis 12:2–3)

13

1. C**H**RIST
2. ST**U**MBLE
3. S**N**ATCHED AWAY
4. WICKE**D** ONE
5. CA**R**ES
6. H**E**ART
7. **D**EPTH
8. **F**RUIT
9. CH**O**KE
10. TRIBU**L**ATION
11. WOR**D** OF GOD

14

15

F**R**EEDOM
FORGIV**E**NESS
CONVICTION
REST**O**RATION
CO**N**FESSION
CREATION
B**I**RTHING
C**L**EANSING
FA**I**TH
RENEW**A**L
REPEN**T**ANCE
SUBM**I**SSION
J**O**Y
U**N**ION

16

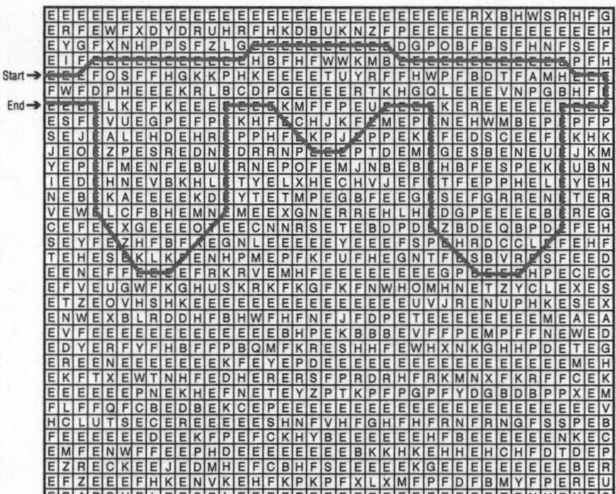

17

5,000 ÷ 10 × 3 ÷ 12 + 38 − 6 + 4 − 1 ÷ 4 − 7 + 2 × 2 = 70

18

Unscrambled letters: A GOOD TESTIMONY

19

Blessed are the merciful, for they shall obtain mercy. (Matthew 5:7)

20

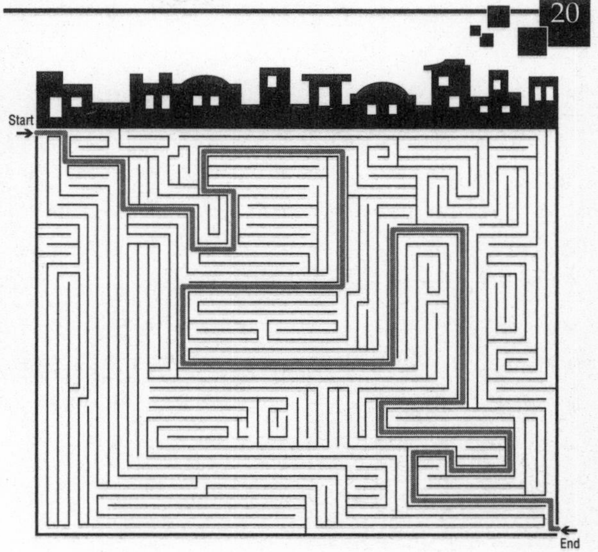

21

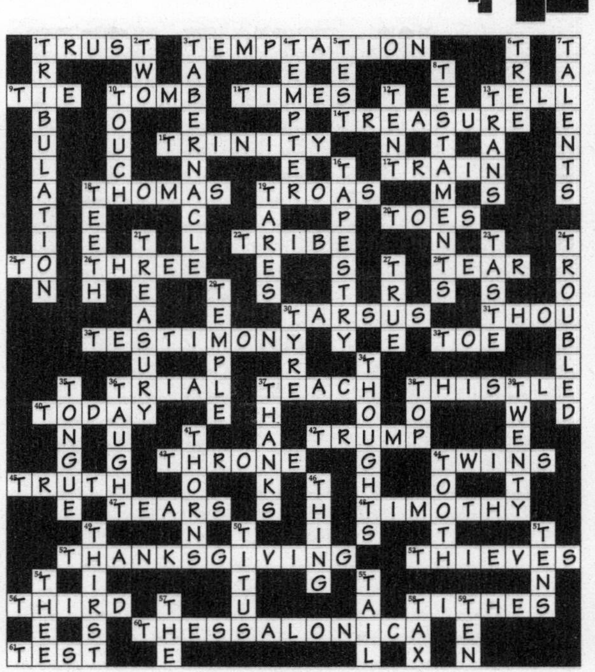

22

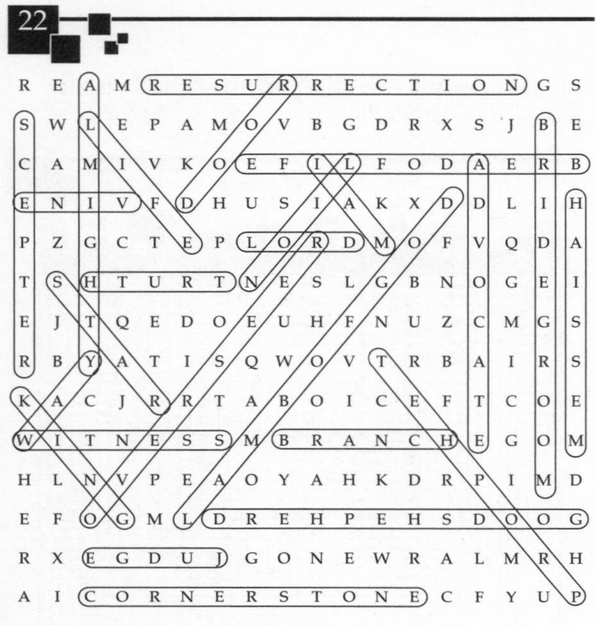

24

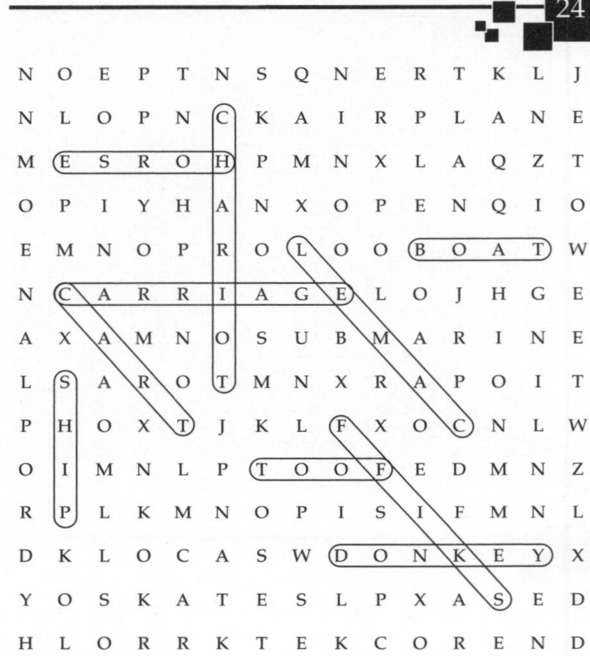

23

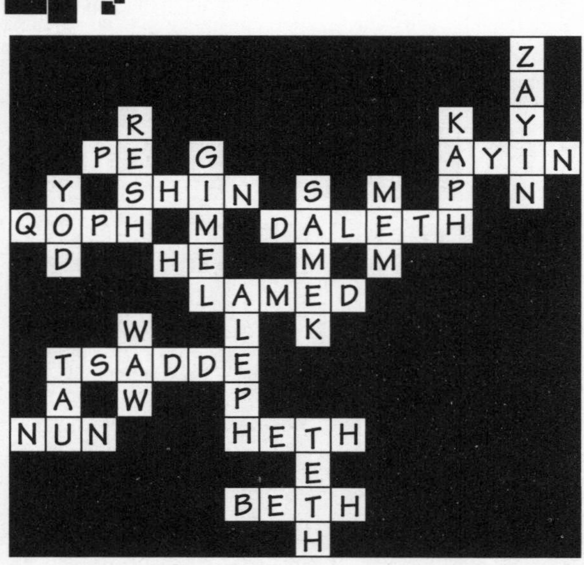

25

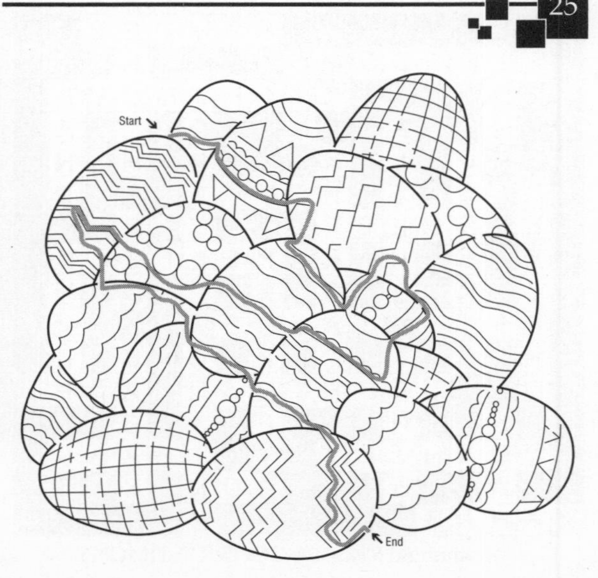

26

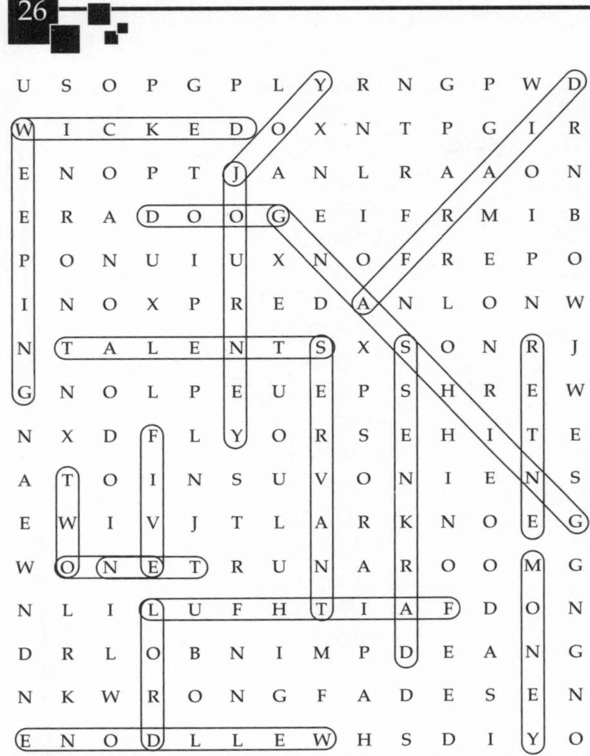

EGYPTIAN S**L**AVERY
MOS**E**S APPOINTED LEADER
PLAGUES AND DEA**T**H OF FIRSTBORN
FREEDO**M**
ACROSS THE RED SEA ON DR**Y** GROUND
PHARAOH DEFEATED
WAT**E**R AND MANNA PROVIDED
M**O**UNT SINAI
REBELLION IN WILDERNESS OF **P**ARAN
40 YEARS IN THE WI**L**DERNESS
CROSSING THE JORDAN RIV**E**R
CONQUERING CANAANITE KIN**G**S
THE PR**O**MISED LAND

LET MY PEOPLE GO

28

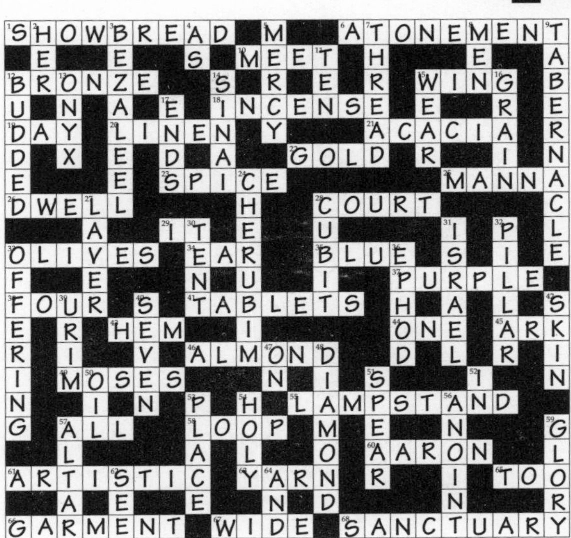

29

E	N	A	E	E	Y	M
E	D	H	D	D	W	N
R	T	T	A	N	O	I
F	H	U	N	I	R	E
U	E	R	D	S	D	D
O	T	T	Y	E	Y	I
Y	R	E	O	L	O	B
E	U	H	U	P	U	A
K	T	T	S	I	A	U
A	H	W	H	C	R	O
M	S	O	A	S	E	Y
L	H	N	L	I	M	F
L	A	K	L	D	Y	I

If you abide in My word, you are My disciples indeed. And you shall know the truth, and the truth shall make you free. (John 8:31–32)

30

32

WATER
EL**I**M
A**L**TAR
CLOU**D**
TRE**E**
MA**R**AH
MAN**N**A
AMAL**E**KITES
SINAI
SIN
PRAYED
OME**R**
BR**O**NZE
AD**V**ANCE
MER**I**BAH
BA**S**HAN
QUA**I**L
H**O**REB
PARA**N**

31

I must work the works of Him who sent me while it is day; the night is coming when no one can work. (John 9:4)

(Begin with the second letter and take every other letter to solve the puzzle. The number reference comes at the end of the string.)

33

34

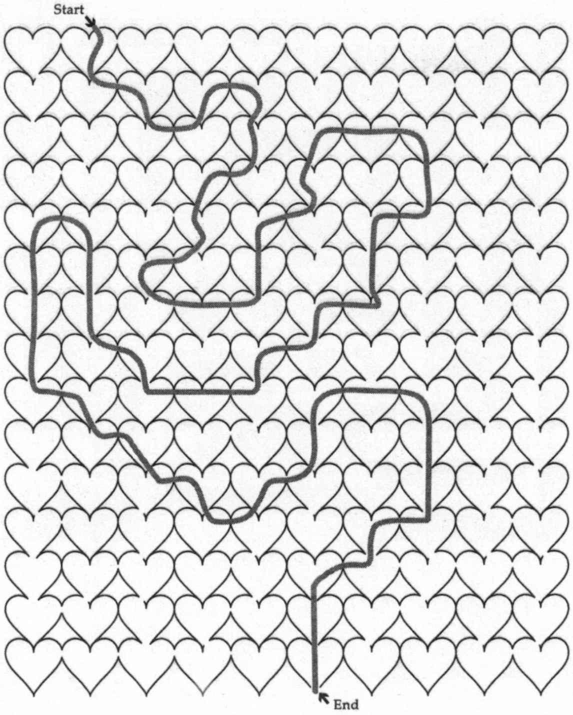

Start

End

36

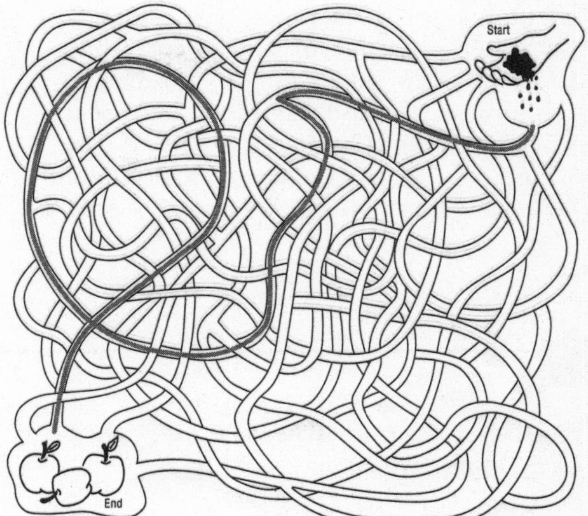

Start

End

35

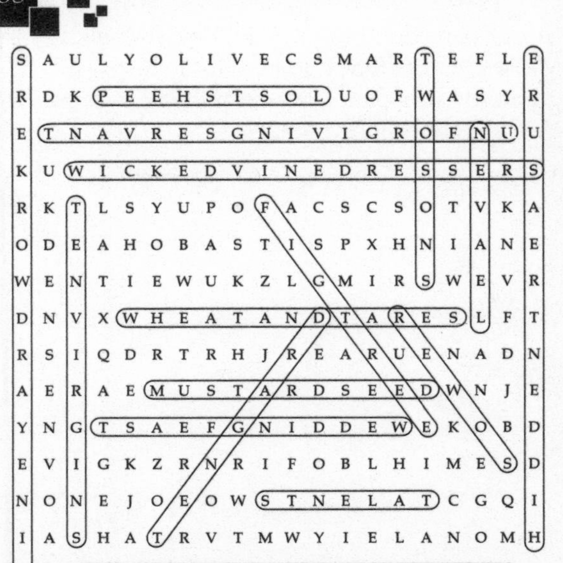

37

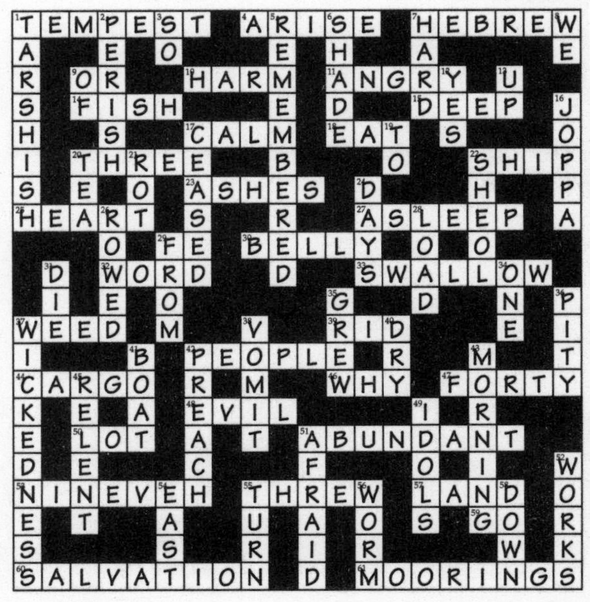

38

1. Cummin	8. Grape	15. Oak
2. Rose	9. Olive	16. Henna
3. Lily	10. Palm	17. Bean
4. Gourd	11. Broom	18. Wheat
5. Mint	12. Aloe	19. Willow
6. Fig	13. Cedar	20. Almond
7. Anise	14. Apple	21. Garlic

42

Bonus: Everywhere

39

Blessed are the pure in heart, for they shall see God. (Matthew 5:8)

40

40 – 5 + 1,260 ÷ 3.5 – 70 ÷ 6 + 17 – 25 – 42 = 0

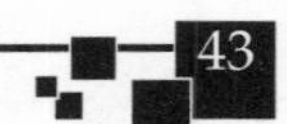

43

Most assuredly, I say to you, he who believes in Me, the works that I do he will do also; and greater works than these he will do, because I go to My Father. (John 14:12)

41

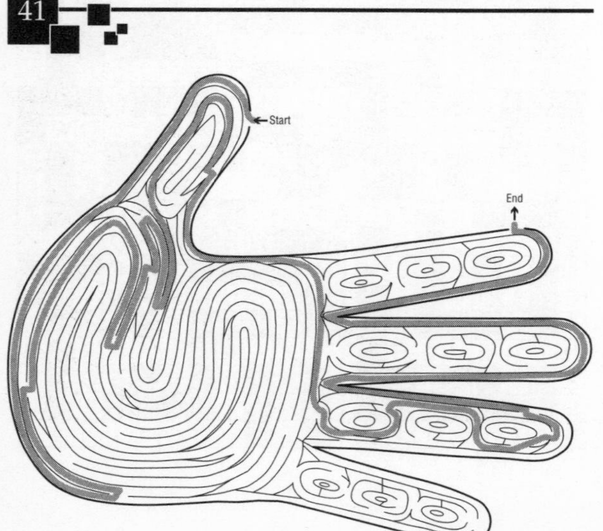

44

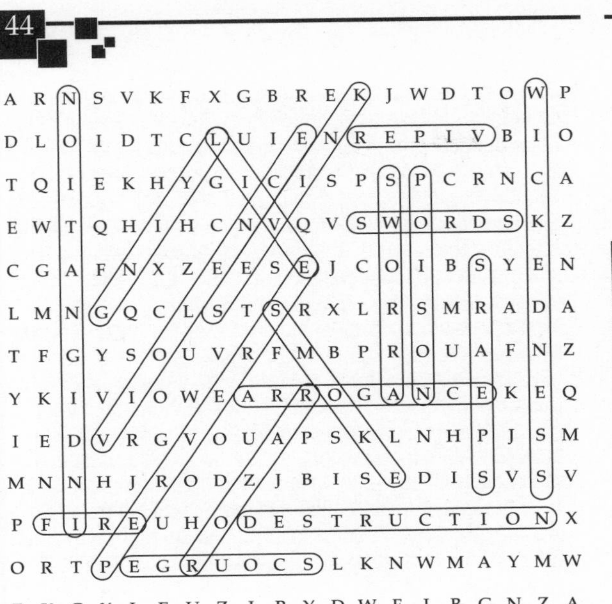

46

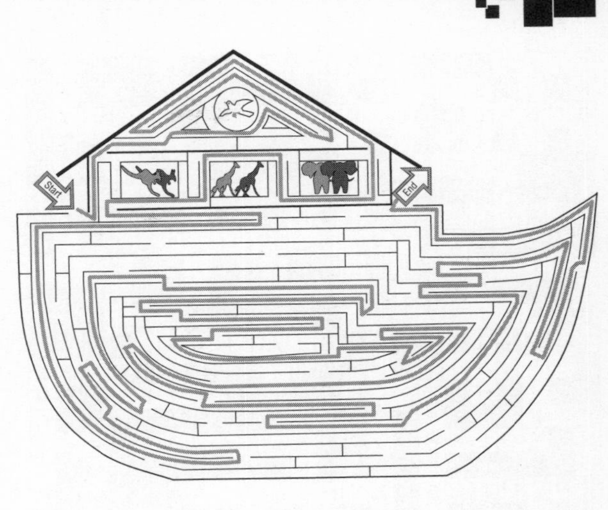

45

Unscrambled letters: The King is coming!

47

Puzzle Answers

48

50

51

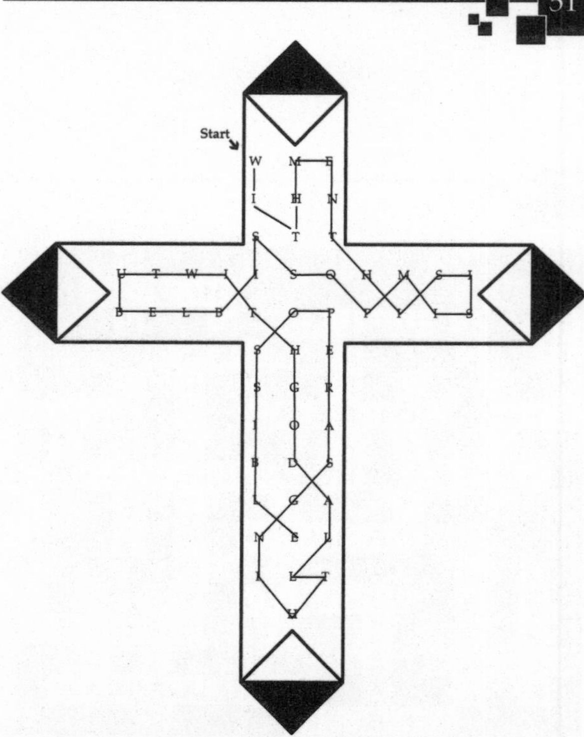

With men this is impossible, but with God all things are possible. (Matthew 19:26)

49

For we do not have a High Priest who cannot sympathize with our weaknesses, but was in all points tempted as we are, yet without sin. Let us therefore come boldy to the throne of grace, that we may obtain mercy and find grace to help in time of need. (Hebrews 4:15–16)

52

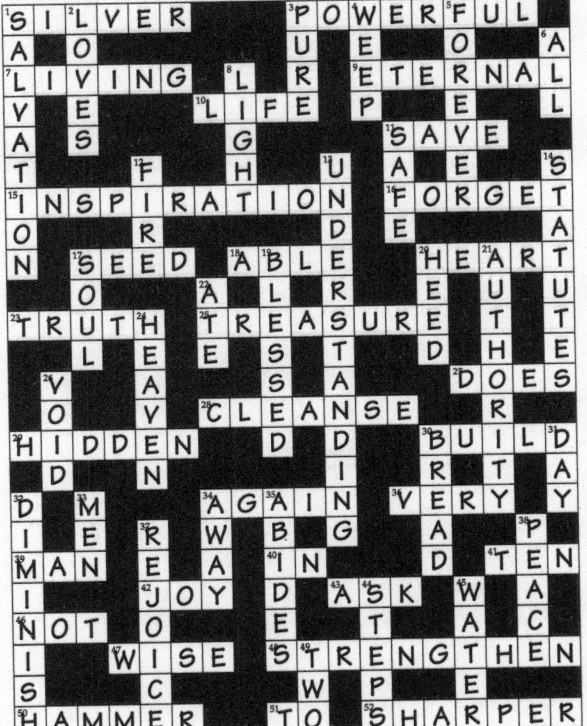

54

Blessed are the peacemakers, for they shall be called sons of God. (Matthew 5:9)

55

53

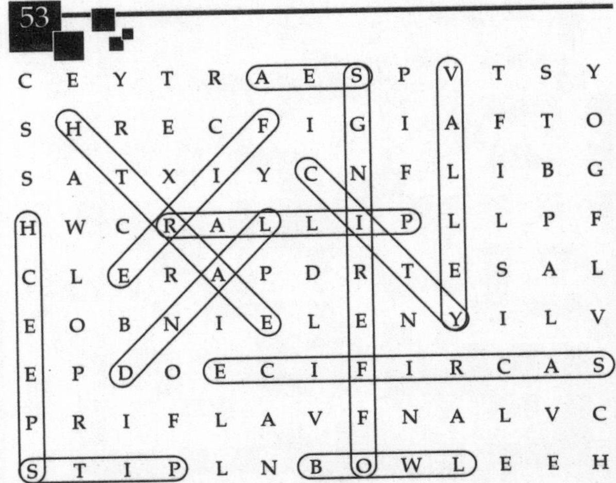

56

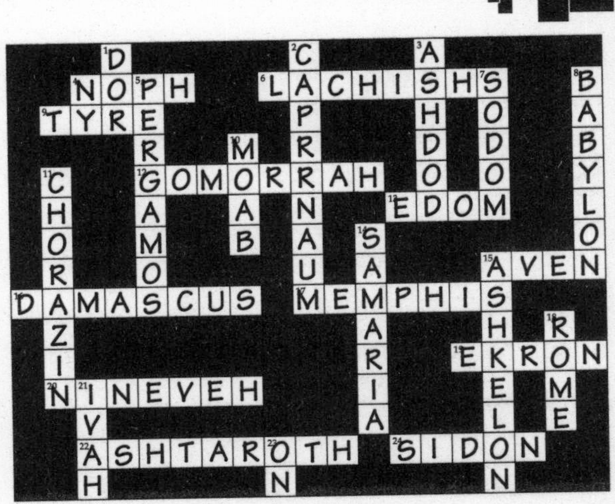

My food is to do the will of Him who sent Me, and to finish His work. (John 4:34)

60

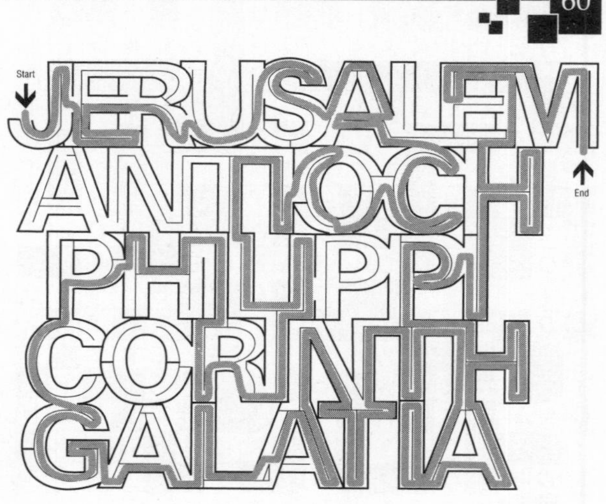

58

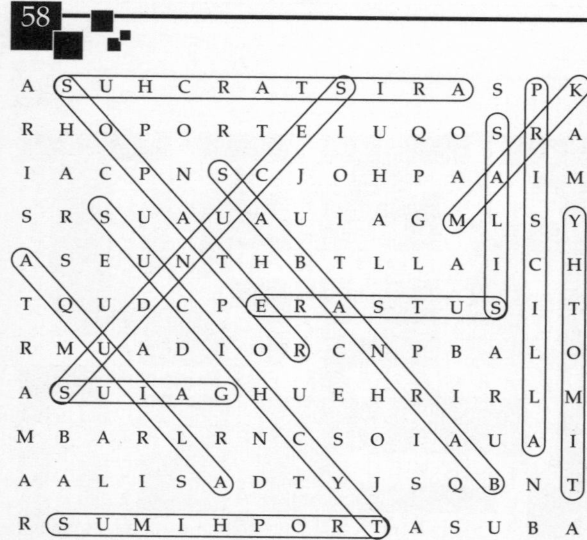

61

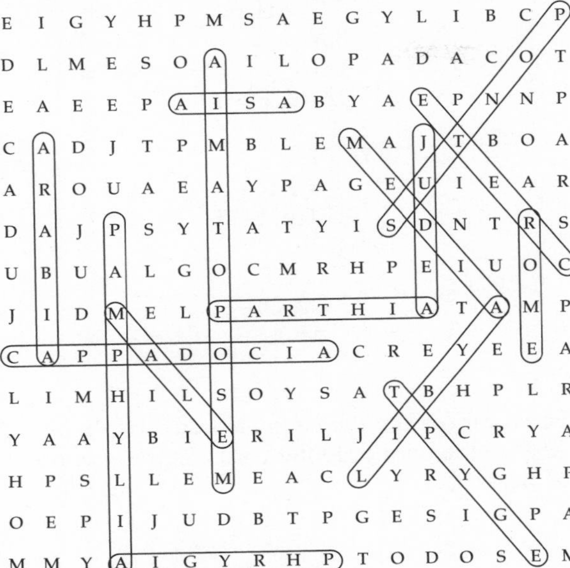

In order to read the words MENE MENE TEKEL UPHARSIN, turn the page on its side! The twenty-one letters of this phrase are in order reading from left to right.

65

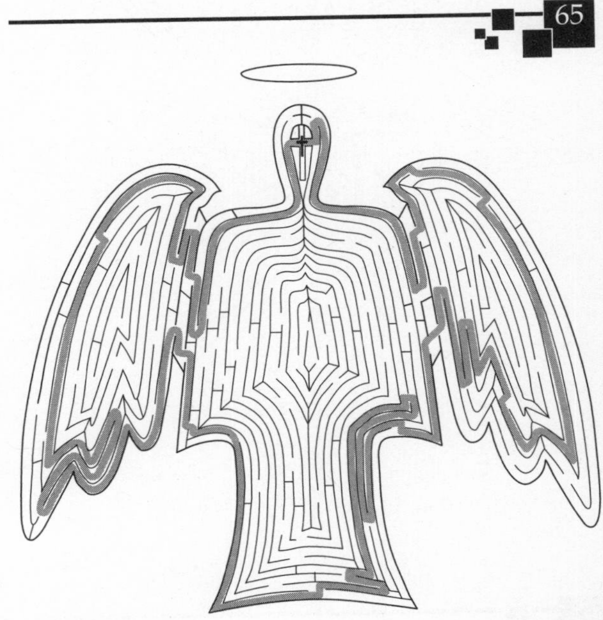

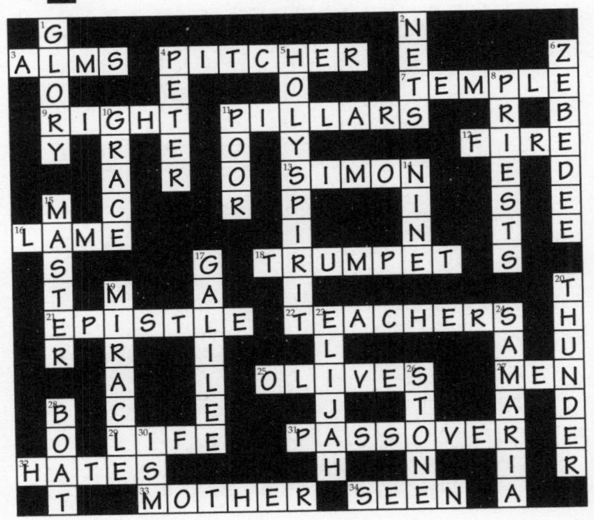

66

MENE: God has numbered your kindgom, and finished it
TEKEL: You have been weighed in the balances, and found wanting
PERES: Your kingdom has been divided, and given to the Medes and Persians

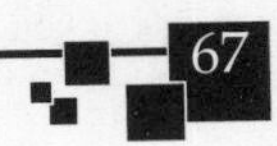

Blessed are those who are persecuted for righteousness' sake, for theirs is the kingdom of heaven. (Matthew 5:10)

68

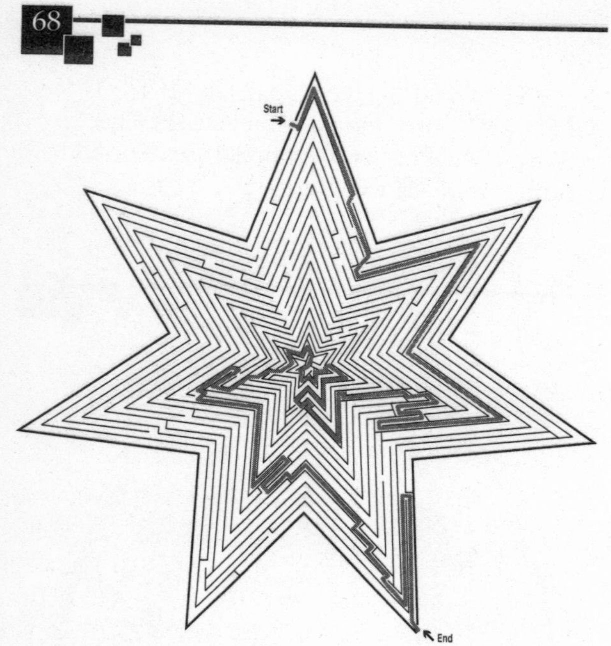

ABRAHAM
ESAU
JACOB
SAMUEL
JOSEPH
ISAIAH
MOSES

JOSEP**H**
ESAU
AB**R**AHAM
SAMU**E**L
ISA**I**AH
J**A**COB
MOSES

Each of these key Bible figures said, "HERE I AM" to the Lord or to the Lord's representative of blessing.

69

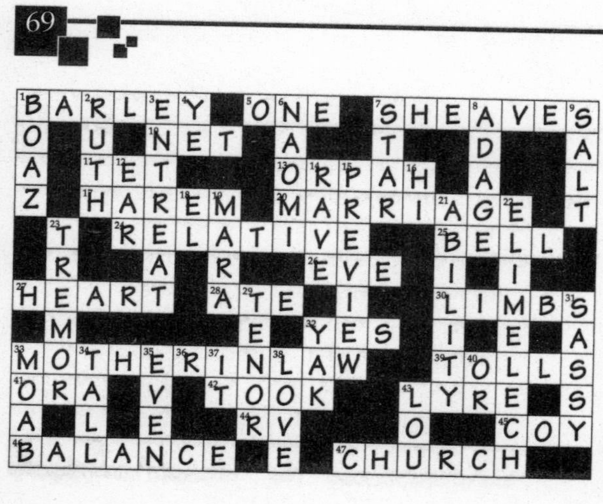

71

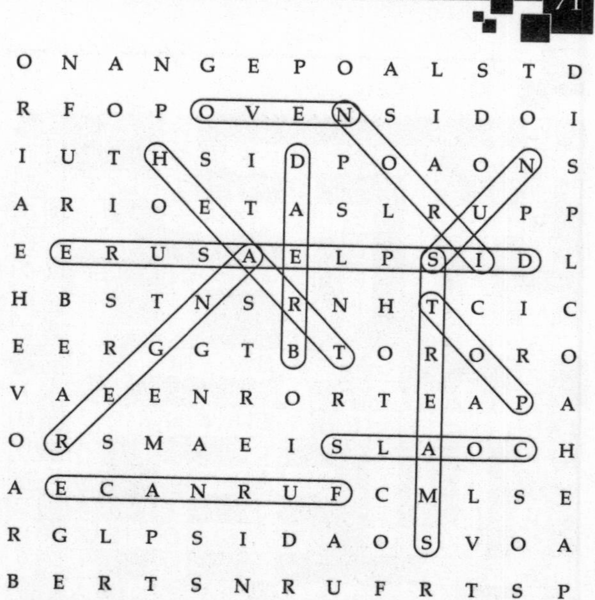

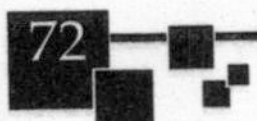

GOOD SHEPHERD

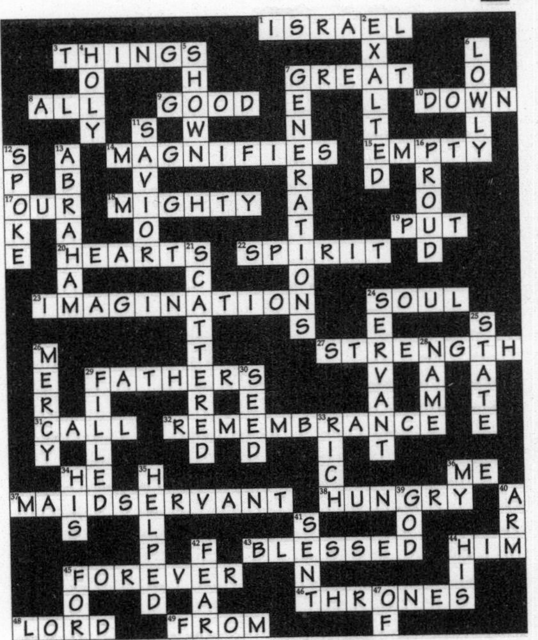

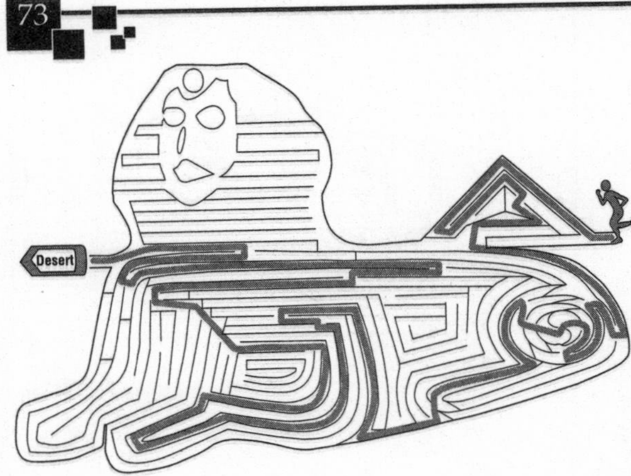

I know your works, that you are neither cold nor hot. I could wish you were cold or hot. So then, because your are lukewarm, and neither cold nor not, I will vomit you out of My mouth. (Revelation 3:15–16)

Each clue letter is two letters behind the actual letter in the verse.

77

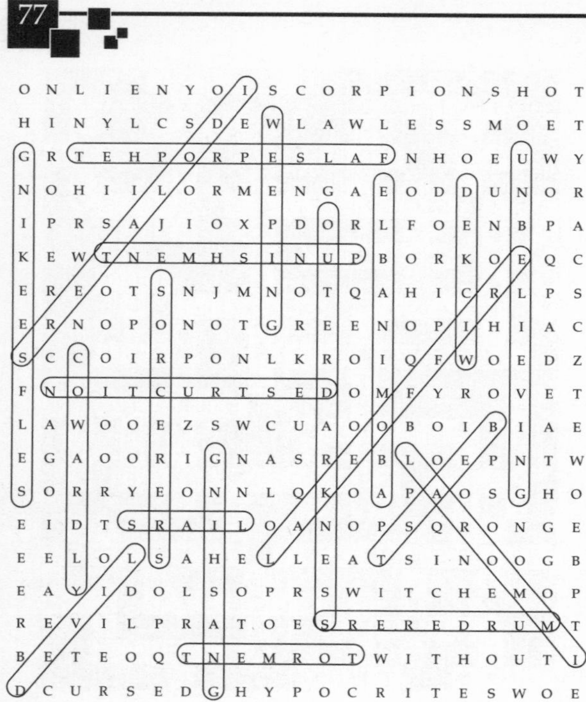

78

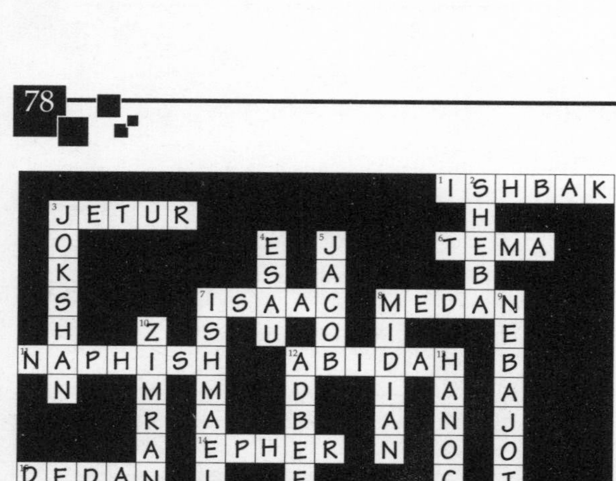

79

80

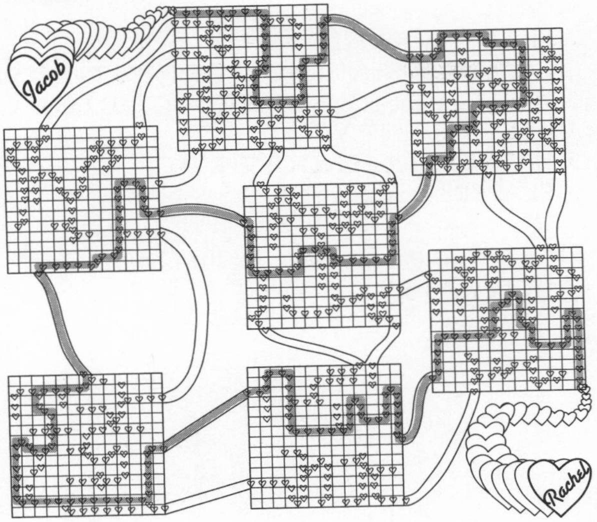

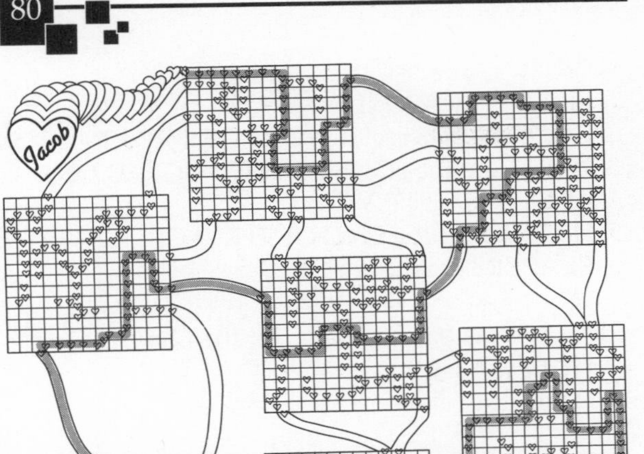

82

If My people who are called by My name will humble themselves, and pray and seek My face, and turn from their wicked ways, then I will hear from heaven, and will forgive their sin and heal their land. (2 Chronicles 7:14)

83

81

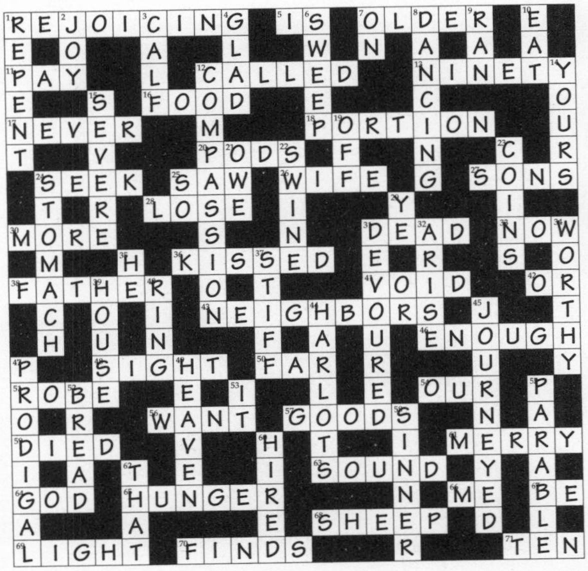

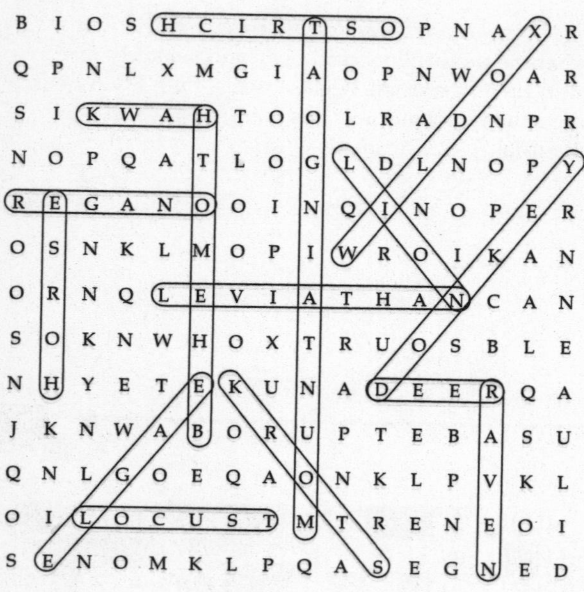

1. FIELD is the WORLD
2. GOOD SEEDS are the SONS OF THE KINDGOM
3. TARES are the SONS OF THE WICKED ONE
4. ENEMY is the DEVIL
5. HARVEST is the END OF THE AGE
6. REAPERS are the ANGELS

He who has ears to hear, let him hear!
(Matthew 13:43)